4th & Inches

A Football Coach's Season Devotional

by John Tomlinson

Cover and illustration design by LaVon Lewis.

For more information, visit coachjohntomlinson.com.

Endorsements for 4th & Inches

"It was an absolute pleasure to have Coach Tomlinson on my staff at Morgan State University. Most young coaches that you hire are eager to show you how much football they know but that was the second thing John wanted to show. The first thing he wanted to show me was his love for being a Christian and his love for God. His approach has helped me to realign my approach to hiring coaches. I want to know what they are willing to stand for before they show me what they know. This helps me to recognize their passion for nurturing and teaching our student-athletes."
Coach Donald Hill-Eley, Head Coach, Alabama State University

"Coach Tomlinson's book provides an incredible resource for coaches to cultivate their faith as they continue to lead young people. Each page is filled with morsels of spiritual nutrition that will empower a coach to walk with conviction and purpose."
Daron K. Roberts, J.D., Founding Director, Center for Sports Leadership & Innovation, University of Texas and Author, "Call An Audible: Let My Pivot from Harvard Law to NFL Coach Inspire Your Transition"

"Having been a player in the NFL, represented NFL athletes (NFLPA) as well as mentor and impact the lives of college student athletes, I believe Coach Tomlinson is on to something powerful. He understands the power of inspiration and its importance to coaches and players from the beginner's coach in high school to the highest level. I've seen the dawn of his process. Somebody will be impacted by this text. JT is a brother, mentor, trusted advisor, and friend!"
Scottie Graham, Senior Associate Athletics director, Arizona State University

"As a child, I attended a YMCA camp that taught campers to live by a simple code, "God first, the other person second, and me third." Coach Tomlinson has written a wonderful guide that brings this truth to life. The nuggets of wisdom contained in ***4th & Inches*** will change your life. Coach John Tomlinson embodies the definition of a winner in every sense of the word."
Dr. Robert W. Turner II, George Washington University School of Medicine and Health Science

"An amazing journey from an amazing man!"
Gerard Wilcher, Rice University, DB Coach

"John is a devoted man of God who has a calling upon his life to lead men. The devotional is a powerful testimonial to his commitment to honor God daily."
Coach Jim Caldwell, Former Head Coach Indianapolis Colts & Detroit Lions

"Few coaches can say they have coached at every single level of football. John Tomlinson has! I have coached 30 years in college and 13 in the NFL and, in all those years, I have worked with no finer Christian man that also has that rare combination of toughness, compassion, and the ability to teach like John. You will want to start your morning with John's new daily devotional ***4th & Inches***!"
David Lee QB Coach, Miami Dolphins, Dallas Cowboys, New York Jets, Buffalo Bills, Cleveland Browns

"We need to own all aspects of our lives. The good, the troubled are to be embraced and treasured. We grow from our experiences in our life's journey which aids in our service to others. This coach's devotional, authored by John Tomlinson, is a testament to his courage, conviction, discipline and most of all abundant patience. We all need to hit the pause and reset button daily, weekly and monthly in our pursuits. ***4th & Inches*** will provide you with an invaluable resource in directing your path and providing you with a new set of downs and attainable goals."
Gene Huey, (Ret.) Indianapolis Colts 1992-2010

"***4th & Inches*** is a must read for every football coach in America! Coach Tomlinson is one of the sharpest football minds in the business. And he's even a better man and Christian. Hit' em hard."
Kirby Wilson RB Coach Arizona Cardinals

"While coaching at the highest level in his sport, the Nation Football League, Coach Tomlinson gave me a unique perspective on football, life and being the best man that I could be. His reliance on faith and family is something that provides strength and guidance during the strenuous times of a football season."
Kevin Hogan, NFL Quarterback

"I've always considered Coach Tomlinson a friend, mentor, and a man of integrity. John is a man of faith who uses football as a teaching tool for life experiences. He has always walked with Christ while inspiring others to aim high and follow their dreams."
Terrence Isaac, Head Coach, Green Oaks Academy H.S., Shreveport, LA

This book has served as a representation of my journey over the last 25 years of pursuing a passion God planted in me at 7 years old.

I'd like to thank those who helped in my process.

I dedicate this book to my late father, Dr. John D. Tomlinson Sr. He told me constantly, as a young man, that I needed to figure out what I wanted to do with my life so I wouldn't have to work five jobs wishing that I'd be doing something I really wanted to do. He was my inspiration as a child and I watched him work day and night so I could have a purpose of my own to pursue one day.

I'd like to thank my wife, Kathy Danielle Tomlinson, who supported this book, my coaching journey, and my passion to take this journey to Texas after the first half of my life coaching. She's been a soldier and the ultimate coach's wife.

To my children for always being supportive and being a part of my process as well. It's a blessing to have awesome children. Raising them has helped me evolve and become a better coach and communicator.

Thank you from the bottom of my heart and soul. ~ John

A special and heart felt thank you to these valuable people.

Vince Bayyan
Coach Brian Braswell
Coach Jim Caldwell
Coach George Collett
Scottie Graham
Pastor Ronnie Henry
Coach Donald Hill-Eley
Coach Gene Huey
Coach Terrence Isaac
Coach David Lee
Aaron and Patrice Marshall
Larry Little
Coach Trei Oliver
Coach Louis Owens
Eric Paul
Coach Frank Reich
Daron Roberts
Nick Savage
Coach Eric Sanders
Coach Al Saunders
Coach Bob Saunders
Justin S'ua
Coach Ricky Thomas
Coach Sam Washington
Coach Marcus White
Coach Kirby Wilson
John Wooten

Thank You

To Coach Donald Hill-Eley for opening a door giving me my first Quarterback Coaching job at the college level. He allowed me to grow and learn how to manage my position group.

To Coach Jim Caldwell for not only giving me my first opportunity in the NFL but meeting with me, listening to my vision for the future, and then following up and hiring me as an intern to begin my NFL career.

To John Wooten for not giving up on me and giving me a chance by calling multiple coaches and general managers encouraging them to consider me for NFL opportunities.

To Coach Gene Huey for being a mentor from the first time I began in the NFL to this very day. You heard my aspirations and never told me to give up. Through each off-season, you've encouraged me to keep pressing while lending your wise perspective.

To Coach Sam Washington and Larry Little for giving me a foundation as a coach. As a 25-year-old coach looking to develop a foundation in the profession and an offensive identity, you both showed me the game through how you communicated and then how you instructed your players.

To Coach Trei Oliver for being a brother and friend as I've endured life and coaching over the last 25 years. You've always been an honest and straightforward brother and a reason you've always been a part of my inner circle.

To Daron Roberts for being a great friend as well as helping me remember that failure is not final and that rejection is just a part of our process. It only takes one.

To Aaron and Patrice Marshall for always being family. Through the life transition after 2003, to the many family adjustments, you guys were always there.

To Scottie Graham for helping me ignite the second phase of my coaching career. Your words of encouragement along with showing me how to take that next step was what I needed. Thanks for being a brother through it all.

To Pastor Ronnie Henry for helping me stay connected to my God-given purpose with your daily encouragement when we were working back in Northern Virginia. You saw it in me every day I came to work and diagrammed plays and talked about game plans. You knew I wouldn't be working in cyber security long. Thanks for seeing it and helping me to trust God's process.

To Coach Ricky Thomas for being a big brother and keeping me encouraged through the many trials that life and coaching has presented me. You stories have been a blessing.

To Frank Reich for being willing enough when I was an intern and very "green" to the NFL to mentor me on the most vital aspects of being a quarterback in the NFL. Thank you also for having the time to share your testimony as a believer and showing me how to manage football and family as a coach.

To Coach Terrence Isaac for propping me up when I couldn't always see the vision I knew God had laid out for me. I appreciate the encouragement as well as being a part of the inner circle.

To Coach Kirby Wilson. Brother, I appreciate your big brother mentoring. You've been a source of inspiration as well as a great teacher in understanding the profession and how to maintain being yourself while growing in this profession.

To Coach David Lee for seeing my potential not only as a quarterback coach but as coach in the NFL. I appreciate your endorsement and willingness to make sure I understood the rigors of the work in the NFL. That will always be appreciated.

To Coach Al Saunders for providing wisdom during my second stint in the NFL. I appreciate you always providing your perspective on the profession and being willing to help me as I adjusted to the speed of the profession.

To Justin S'ua for being an open ear while I was in Cleveland. Each week, I appreciated the wisdom that you led the team inspirationals with. Your positive outlook on life helped me understand that I was on the right path.

Thank you to all those pivotal people I may have not listed specifically. I'm appreciative to all everyone who helped me stay grounded and who reminded me to never give up.

Introduction

On September 10, 2017, you couldn't have scripted a better day to play a football game. As I peaked out the window from my room early that morning at the team hotel, I saw the beautiful Lake Erie water cradle the stadium we were about to play in. I anticipated this opening day game as if it was Christmas morning when I was a child. Everything for me, building up to my short drive to the stadium, was pure anticipation for our week 1 game at home. As I later flashed my coaching credentials and went through security at the stadium, I knew I had crossed another level in life that I'd been pursuing for more than 10 of the 25 years that I'd been coaching.

During our pre-game warm-up routine, I spotted my wife in the stands waving at me and a calm fell over me. As I took in the subtle breeze from Lake Erie, I could smell the faint aroma from the polish sausages and onions nearby. My eyes began to water, but not because of the food, rather for the gratefulness I felt to be in this moment.

To be in this stadium and look at the amazingly blue sky and absorb the perfect 70+ degree temperatures, there wasn't much that could rival this moment.

The surreal emotions continued in the press box before kickoff. As I had prepared my two pens, two pencils, 1st and 2nd half play-script templates, I was in tune and prepared for our head coach to make his first offensive call of the game. When I gazed out into the sea of black and gold Steeler fans mixed in with ripples of brown and orange, I imagined my dad sitting up in the highest part of the First Energy Stadium seats eating peanuts and drinking a 32 oz cup of beer telling everyone within earshot, "That's my son, my son coaches with the Cleveland Browns. Yep, that's my boy. I'm proud of him." I could almost hear him saying that as he'd continue to deshell and eat his peanuts and take down his beer. After losing my father two months prior to this opening day game, I knew he was in the stadium to help indoctrinate my first regular season game as a NFL coach. This was truly my finest day in the profession and it was represented throughout my 25 years with endurance, blood, sweat and tears.

In 1994, my life was transformed when I accepted my first coaching position at Cardinal Gibbons High School in Raleigh, NC. I was introduced to my purpose after four years of hard work pursuing my undergraduate degree in Computer Science. Yes! I said it… Computer Science! At that time in my life, I was all about pursuing the best financial opportunity. I thought stepping into technology was the best choice to get an education and pursue a career (and the money). Making big money drove me and Information Technology at that time was the way to do it.

Fast forward to our world currently, I believe I was correct in choosing to pursue my passion. My passion for the game had a hold on me and it started when I was a little boy in the 70s watching the Dallas Cowboys play on Sundays with my dad. I was fixated on the TV. Nothing could pull me away. I would go outside and play one-on-one with myself. I'd be on defense and then offense, switching back and forth until I narrated a complete game. From the first pair of white cleats my dad bought me at age 11, until now as a coach who breaks down film and evaluates QBs and defensive tendencies, the love for the game has been a part of me.

Well, a year after my first coaching assignment, I realized that I might have missed my true calling while I was a student at Winston-Salem State University. Coaching became my lifeblood, my thirst quencher, and the thing I chased from that point forward. It's been 24 years since that first coaching job. I've had the chance to grow in this profession. I've had the opportunity to coach at every level of football. Those opportunities have been the most humbling and most rewarding experiences for me; to see every level of football from Pop Warner, high school, college, all the way to the National Football League (NFL).

Through each of the years that I've coached, I've learned how important God has been in my journey. Having integrated God in my position meetings and in my relationships with my position group, has helped me in how I deal with fans, parents, fellow coaches, my wife and how I approach my personal preparation. Integrating God in my everyday coaching responsibilities has helped me maintain balance or, as I've heard a few older and wise coaches say to me over the years, "keep the main thing, the main thing."

I've spent a lot of time in a variety of head coaches' offices over the years and, in almost

all of them, I saw a fair share of devotionals sitting on the table next to the coach's phone or keyboard. It was an integral part of how that coach approached his day. God has imparted upon me the same ability to create a devotional for my brothers in this profession. This devotional is a weekly guide created specifically for you that is filled with key principles, questions and reminders as you step through your 24-week season. If you think about all the work you do from late July to early February, no matter if you are a high school, college, or professional coach, you are constantly being pulled in multiple directions and sometimes don't have that time to pause. It is my hope that this book will give you a chance to pause for a few minutes daily and create some time with you and God to help you enhance your weekly game plan. There's no better Owner-General Manager then God Himself to hold you accountable every day.

From my time as Quarterback Coach, Offensive Coordinator, and Offensive Quality Control in college and the NFL, I gained more clarity on life and my job the more I involved God during each week of the season.

It is my hope that you enjoy this walk with God throughout your season. We always need Him. Integrating Him into our full process is what we will walk through, together, in this devotional. Let's get this season started off right!

Table of Contents

The Principles

It's true that almost every coach that has coached for any length of time and has experienced some success with impacting lives, has been regulated by a set of principles or core beliefs. I will present two very valuable beliefs in the next few pages that I'd like to add to your weekly coach's study as you set out to determine the type of organization, coaching staff and players you are a part of.

1) Four Types of Commitment
2) The Sponge and the Brick

Before we dive into the "The Principles," let me first share my thoughts on what it's like to be a part of this coaching fraternity. Simply put, it's much like a marriage where you bring in your pre-existing habits, baggage, differences, upbringing, pains, passions, and optimism. As the pastor prepares a congregation for a bride's march down the aisle on her wedding day, that's exactly what you're doing when you enter the doors of the building upon being hired. In no way am I saying you'll be wearing a wedding dress, but once you walk through these doors, you're going to go through a series of thoughts to recognize if there's a true fit and if the culture suits who you are. While you're going through that, the head coach who has created the culture is processing the same thoughts about you and each individual in the building from player to coach.

As I've grown over the years as a coach, I've brought my childhood, my upbringing, and my straightforward, military-style Marine Corps father right along with me. I've brought my wounds as well. As I've grown, I've identified how to get the most out of each player that I've been privileged to mentor, coach, and father. If it wasn't for my baggage and all my experiences, I'm not sure that I would've been as effective as a coach. The things we bring, our unique experiences, aren't counter productive but rather useful and that's why God has placed us strategically in the places we are today so He can get the glory from the lessons we bring and share with our peers and players. Let's get started on this journey and talk about "The Principles" in the next few pages.

Principle One

Four Types of Commitment

Years ago, I heard a pastor speak on the three types of Christians in today's church. From his message, I was inspired to create the four types of commitment noticed from a coach and player. I began to use it when talking to our players during every off-season before we headed into spring ball. I categorized players into one of four categories, as you will see.

Principle 1, #1: The Ankle Deep Player

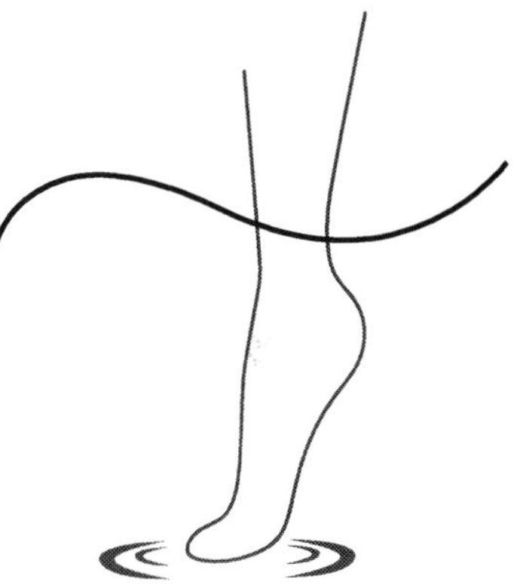

This is a player who, most honestly, doesn't belong in the program. I coined the acronym for this type of guy as a D.B., which means that he doesn't belong. He is not consistent, not committed, and typically not available. He's the player signed to the 90-man roster, the camp body only needed to provide reps and protection for the players that are staying. When the cuts occur, he's the first gone. There isn't enough there and it's all defined in his body language and lack of commitment. As the illustration conveys, he just wants to get his feet wet, but not submerge himself into the process. Not willing to be all in. He only wants to touch the "golden ring" and as soon as he does, he's not willing to put in the time to work for the ring. In the high school ranks, this is the kid that doesn't make it to the first scrimmage because he can't endure the workouts and didn't show up all summer. In the college ranks, this is the guy who tries out as a walk-on and makes it past the first day, but doesn't show up for the second day. "Hey man, that's too much, I'm good!" I think you get the point.

Principle 1, #2: The Knee Deep Player

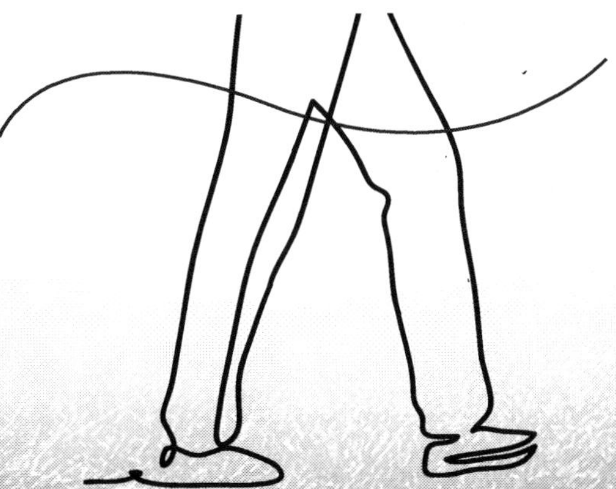

This is a player who has the ability. He simply gets in his own way so often that he can't help himself elevate. When tough times hit, he doesn't hit back. He's a Tuesday player with the unwillingness to risk making Wednesday a follow-up day to a fine performance. In many ways, he's a Below Average Dude (or B.A.D. as

the acronym conveys) but not bad in the proverbial good way on the field or off. His vices in his mind make him unable to want to compete at a high level. Much of that is due to his immaturity. As a coach, you have to find a way to mend the mendable and get this young man to produce consistently by stringing together small victories, which will lend to his success. Upon evaluating this player, he's barely a 50-50 guy. If you were a pro scout, one of the words that would associate with his game day performance would be "erratic" or "inconsistent" with "moments of brilliance." In the old adage of less is more, the less of this type of player you have on the team, the better.

Principle 1, #3: The Waist Deep Player

This is a player who has more than just ability; he's shown he can make plays. However, in the most critical moments, he doesn't produce. During a typical practice week in the NFL, he's great on Wednesday and Thursday, but on Sunday what looked routine on Thursday seems now to be an arduous task for him. He's slightly untimely to the install meetings to start the week and he lacks the discipline to be the complete player his ability conveys that he should be. He's typically incomplete because of what's between his ears. When the going gets tough, he leaves the building. When the sun is shining, he's all in; when it's torrential rain and we're down late in the game and he hasn't produced the entire game, he's "Checkout Charlie." His mind has left the building. He's considered a 50-50 guy or an Average Ass Dude (A.A.D). He has everything needed to be great except for, wait for it…belief in himself! Coach, you will experience a "Waist Deep" player. This is the ingredient in every program that doesn't make the bowl game, loses in the first round of the high school playoffs, or doesn't advance to the playoffs in the NFL. There are too many "Waist Deep" players AND "Waist Deep" coaches. Great coaches help produce and pull out the best from players and coaches with a waist deep mindset.

Principle 1, #4: The Submerged Player

This is a player who is all in with his responsibility to "serve" the team. He's committed and because of his commitment, he excels on and off the field. He serves his teammates

and helps the player behind him on the depth chart because, quite frankly, it helps him retain knowledge of his assignment. He is unselfish and unrelenting in his job. He's sold out, committed, and buries himself in his playbook. When he's in high school or college, he's an honor roll student, academic All American and no one ever questions his classroom work ethic because his results speak for themselves. He's a student of the game, a student of his position and a teacher to his peers. He holds himself accountable as well as his teammates. If the coach is late to the field because of a meeting, this committed player is leading his position group. This player may not have started as a submerged player but he matured into one.

Coach, it's our job to remember the four types of commitment and identify, evaluate, and shape our players weekly as you'll see in your devotional.

Principle #2

The Sponge & Brick

From the very first day you walk into almost any football program, an observation will be made determining what type of player or coach you are going to be. You are either "A Sponge" or "A Brick." You will have a choice, but only one of these will produce results that will lead the team and that same result will produce respect, admiration by your peers, and a humility that will allow you to live a life that constantly produces positive results. Review the attributes below and determine where you stand and where you're willing to go.

VS.

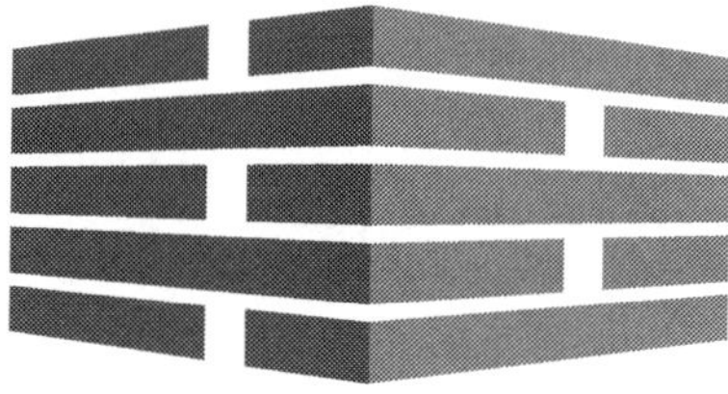

Attributes

Sponge	Brick
Weight **Light, Permeable**	**Weight** **Heavy, Dense**
Mobility **Quick, Good body movement**	**Mobility** **Slow, good in one direction, Can't get out of his own way**
Skill **Adapts well, responds to opponent's style, Moldable, Teachable**	**Skill** **Not adaptable, one way, one style but hard & powerful, Stubborn, can't be broken, can't see it any other way**
Intangible **Uncanny ability to learn and soak up information as fight carries on. Knows when to take information and when to repel bad information**	**Intangible** **Wears the world on his shoulders when he's hurt, When he's broken, the damage is evident to everyone. Not easily broken but when he is, he's hard to get back on track**

Remember this, bricks are meant for building tall structures, homes, banks, and malls, not for building the hearts of men.

Think about when you crack a brick with a hammer, when you put it back together the crack still shows. Much like a hard-hearted man, once scarred, the wound shows and is a reminder of the unwillingness to be transformed. Bricks aren't permeable; they can't soak up the fountain of wisdom. If you poured into a brick, it's too dense to receive what you pour into it. It simply bounces off.

All that I mentioned about the brick, is completely opposite of the sponge. A sponge is light weight, not hard hearted. You can penetrate it with wisdom and it will soak up every ounce and disperse or pass its wisdom on to someone else. If it absorbs something toxic, it can be removed, squeezed out and cleansed. It can be taken to the fountain of wisdom and be restored. It can remove its stains by soaking itself with newness.

As you proceed, think about the type of player you are working to produce, coach, and develop. Think about the type of coach you must be in order to reach a sustainable level of success. It doesn't come without a willingness to seek the fountain of wisdom.

Remember the Reminders

The reminders here will help you through the tough weeks leading up to game day. They will serve as accountability checkpoints throughout the week. On every level of football the only difference is when the game is played. Around that game, the week is broken into:

A. Game Planning
B. Scouting Report
C. Player Day Off
D. Game Plan Install & Practice
E. Walk Through
F. Game Day
G. Post-Game & On to the Next One!

Having lived the life of a QB Coach and Offensive Coordinator at the high school level, a QB Coach and Quality Control Coach at the college level, and an Assistant to the QB Coach and Quality Control Coach in the NFL, I've found that balance is required on every level. Reminding myself of that daily was absolutely mission critical! When I forgot, that was the moment that I became stressed. Over the years, I've learned to break my week down and compartmentalize my work. Let me remind you of the three elements below, which helped me better deal with coaches around me as well as the players. Let's install the following principles into your weekly flow:

1) Power Of Words, Temperament
2) The "Old Iso" Play (Who's Leading?)
3) Don't Worry About Vulnerability

I will break each one down so as you see these reminders weekly in your workbook section after each devotional, you'll liken them to plays off of your call sheet on your weekly practice script or game day sheet. When you see them hopefully they'll bring immediate recognition to what they mean to you as you go through your week.

Remember #1: The Power of Words

Story:

For well over 30 of the 47 years of life I've lived so far, I've studied my earthly father. Some of my habits, sense of humor, and smile have been credited by many as being from the "Old Man," my dad. I've learned over time what has made my dad tick, what has hurt him and what has troubled his soul.

For the last 10 years of his life, my dad dealt with dementia and a long track record of poor health. It truly has been one of the most troubling things to watch. Prior to his dementia, I saw the things in his life that broke him.

It all started with his words. For years, my dad was broken from a failed marriage, a few relationships that followed, missed opportunities in his career and so on. He constantly reiterated his words of personal failure. His lack of forgiving himself and moving on to a better life filled with God's great expectations made him withdraw from those who loved and supported him. "Son, I don't care if you find me in a gutter or dead in my home. That's just where you'll find me." Those were some of the last words he expressed to me months before he was found dead in his home.

I remember almost every single lesson and his constant bluntness. He ran a hard race in this life, never realizing his greatness and how well built for life's challenges he was because he let his words defeat him. It's been a year since his death, but this particular lesson has stuck with me the most. For the greater portion of my young life, I saw women come and go in our home due to his failed attempts at some stability while trying to give me the mom I didn't have as a kid. He really tried and I credit him for his efforts. What he didn't realize, beyond wanting companionship, is that he already was blessed beyond measure. He raised a coach, a soldier, a strong father and a husband all by himself. He worked three jobs, was a Marine and an Army veteran having served in Vietnam and Guantanamo Bay. My dad was awarded a Purple Heart and a National Defense Service Medal. He was a dedicated police officer and a devoted father who did everything possible to make sure I had what I needed. He had already won in life, but his words took away the victories.

Remember Reminder #1: The Power of Words, Temperament

Your words have power. The things you say, what you convey in regards to your body language, and what you believe about your players and coaches are a direct reflection of your belief system. Negative words impact the psyche of your belief system. They tear down what God has built up. Your words can be a contradiction to what He has built up.

As it says in Ephesians 4:29, *"Let no corrupting talk come out of your mouths, but only such as is good for building up, as fits the occasion, that it may give grace to those who hear."*

The words that come out of your mouth have a direct reflection on your response and behavior. As was the case with my dad, his words came true. Although it was tough to see my dad go through so many struggles, he got exactly what he spoke.

God has provided us an abundant life that first starts with our words. As was the case with my dad, it's important to remember, it all started with his words. Whether it's towards yourself or toward someone else, be mindful of your words and the power they possess. There is indeed power in your words. Use words that speak of victory over your past defeats and not negativity or fear. Winning the "word war" in your souls is the first place you have to start... meaning and believing words of increase and victory. Remind yourselves of this scripture that talks about the power of your words as well.

Proverbs 18:4 The words of a man's mouth are deep waters. Wisdom comes like a flowing river making a pleasant noise.

Let go walk and talk with power!

Remember Reminder #2: The "Old Iso" Play (Who's Leading?)

Story:

In 2001, I was the Offensive Coordinator and QB Coach at what was considered a doormat football program at Falls Church High School in Falls Church, VA. Falls Church was primarily known for its soccer excellence as opposed to football. The last winning

season the football team had was in the mid 80s and this was my first opportunity since leaving North Carolina to be an Offensive Coordinator again.

Going into the season, I liked the idea of being King David in a world of Goliaths. There wasn't a soul that gave us a chance. Coaches warned me before taking the job to walk away. They conveyed to me that this job would be a coach killer. I didn't see that; I saw God's value in the opportunity. I saw God's increase in taking this job and I knew He would take me to another level if I took what other coaches saw as a risk. The head coach had a vision and needed support. We were fortunate to have had a great offensive Line and a big RB and FB. The play of choice going into the season was the "Old Iso" play. The Iso has famously been the play where the FB isolates on the Inside Linebacker. There's a double team on the tight shade or one technique by the weak side guard and center versus a traditional 4-3 over front while the weak side tackle turns out the defensive end. We tricked this play up in every way imaginable. We shifted and motioned to get the ideal look and every time we studied film, we'd smile when getting an even front team to play against.

We started the season out with a squatty, 210-pound FB who would put his Schutt sticker on the chest of the Inside Linebacker. This play turned around our team's fortune along with a 195-pound HB. We finished the season 6-4. It was the first winning season the program had in quite a while! Two years later, I was fortunate to be blessed with another talented HB and FB. In 2003, I was the Offensive Coordinator and QB Coach at Parkview High School in Sterling, VA. I fondly remember we had a talented young freshman HB that was an expert at running Power and the "Old Iso" play. He had a low center of gravity, he was physical, and he had a feel for the crease and a trust in his fullback. As a freshman HB, he ran for over 1,700 yards. There was no expectation in the area that this kid would have been that successful, but he believed in not only his ability, but in the fullback that lead for him. The entire year, we ran an up-tempo multiple "I" formation offense that predicated its success on getting lined up properly and trusting the legs of our freshman running back running the "Old Iso" play.

The strength of the "Old" Iso play wasn't just the HB, but it was the trust in the FB leading up on the inside linebacker. As often as possible, we must remember Jeremiah

29:11. We have to remind ourselves that God is our lead FB. He already subscribed a plan specifically for us. The chaos, the adversity and challenges that we face are all preparation for the plans He has for us. In Jeremiah 29:11, God says, *"For I know the thoughts that I think toward you, saith the Lord, thoughts of peace, and not of evil, to give you an expected end."* We have to simply trust our lead blocker that's isolating on our destiny that was prepared for us a long time ago. Sometimes we forget that He's already got a plan for us. The "Iso" play, unlike years ago, isn't run as much. But when it is, the man that's relied upon for success is the FB. Visualize that FB being God Himself. He's your lead blocker, protector, care provider and bodyguard. You are the HB! All you have to do is keep your eyes on Him or as we would teach years ago, "HB, read the back of the FB's helmet." No matter how you teach the "Old" Iso play, remember to keep your eyes fixed on God and simply let Him lead.

A Pause Before Remember Reminder #3

In 2011, I got a call from the Cleveland Browns based on a referral from a mentor of mine who recommended me for a potential position that he deemed would help the team as well as my growth. It was a late summer flight and my optimism was high for an opportunity to be in the NFL again.

Upon meeting the Head Coach, my first impression was hopeful and he asked me where I visualized myself in five years. I told him I'd like to be assisting a position coach on the field. After spending five hours with the team and preparing to go home, he told me they wouldn't create the position, so I flew home disappointed and desperate to change the course for my life.

It's highly likely that my answer to his question wasn't the one he wanted to hear but I didn't know it was an incorrect answer. After serving the previous summer in Indianapolis learning from Coach Jim Caldwell's staff, I was hoping this was the bridge to grow in the NFL. As I flew back home, I couldn't visualize providing for my family for another year as a substitute teacher while having already sacrificed a six-figure salary to pursue this mission of coaching in the NFL or college, so I called a friend who I use to work for as a federal government contractor in the Washington, D.C. area. He hired me immediately and I headed back to the east coast.

Upon arriving in DC, I spent the fall as an offensive consultant with a local high school team. Early in the winter of 2012, I received a call from an old friend that was coaching at Morgan State University as the Linebacker Coach. He knew I was seeking to grow in my career and he kept me updated on any coaching opportunities he'd hear about. Coach Don Hill at Morgan State University was seeking an assistant QB coach and after a 30-minute sit down with Coach Hill, he offered me the job. He heard my passion and was willing to help me grow in my career.

A month after I started at Morgan State, Coach Hill's QB Coach left the staff and he immediately told me without hesitation that he was promoting me and had already evaluated my work ethic and how I communicated. From one situation that seemed to be disappointing, another door opened and someone was willing to help me by offering me an opportunity. "All that I ask of you is that when you're in a position to help someone else on your career path, you do so. This would be the ultimate payback or pay it forward for me," said Coach Hill after he promoted me.

I did all that I could to make sure I was on top of my role at Morgan State from recruiting to taking care of my position group. I had a local apartment near the university while still working in Northern Virginia, contracting for the federal government. My schedule consisted of waking up at 2:30 a.m. and taking a 40 minute drive to Reston, VA, starting at 4:30 a.m. and leaving work at 2:30 p.m. everyday so I could be at practice at 3:20 p.m. I prepared all my meals and ironed all my clothes for the week on Sunday. I was not deterred by lack of sleep. I did my recruiting calls and texts in the evenings after practice and broke down practice film before bed. I managed everything inside of a four-hour window after practice and I worked to get in the bed by 11 p.m. each night. My desire to thrive in this profession fed me while I went through this stage in life. I learned a lot at Morgan State in my year and a half, but family priorities required a change.

Remember Reminder #3: Don't Worry About Vulnerability

In the summer of 2013, I was prepping my car for the long 19-hour drive back to Dallas from Baltimore. I made a family decision to return Texas after a modest first season as an FCS QB Coach and Offensive Quality Control Coach. I say modest because the program

was in a rebuilding phase and we lost some close games in the 2012 season with a string of young QBs.

The greatest highlight from the previous season that fueled 2013 optimism was our recruiting class. Between the head coach and myself, we recruited a quality group of student athletes from Texas and Oklahoma. While I recruited North Texas, the head coach recruited the southern part of the state. There was some excitement heading into the season and I felt some purpose, but the calling to go home to be closer to family was strong. I was already away for two years since the job rejection in Cleveland and I had put some money away working again in Northern Virginia as a contractor. My wife wanted me home. I could hear it in her voice with every conversation we had as I headed toward the end of the spring semester; she was missing me more than ever.

I took the risk and felt in some ways that I was slowing down my college coaching momentum. I had also built some trust and rapport with Coach Hill and struggled with this move because he gave me this opportunity, but I didn't want to be a failed marriage statistic. I arrived in Texas in mid-July and took a coaching job at a nationally-ranked high school football program. As tough as it was, I put my focus on the next move before I even started this job. While doing that, I refused to become the servant I long remembered I was taught to be. I didn't want to become vulnerable to the coaches or the players in the program. I was only looking for the exit. I had the "one and done" mentality. I missed the college game and the pageantry of Saturday afternoons. I certainly didn't have the best mindset heading into the fall.

As I progressed through the start of the season, (and actually from the very beginning in August) I was tasked with managing the middle school program and assisting in the afternoons with the high school program. How humbling this experience was! I was previously traveling, coaching, and recruiting on the college level and basking in the excitement of Saturday afternoon games.

I was hit with a strong tide of humility one day when reporting to work. I realized I had purpose in coming back to the high school level and it was apparent early one morning when a young 7th grader reported to practice at 6:30 a.m. telling me, "Coach, I want to

go to the NFL. I know we start practice at 7:15, but I wanted to come early to study some plays. Can you show me what I'm supposed to do on these plays?" as he pointed to the diagram that I had on the board in the locker room. Although this was a tough stretch for me and my desire to get back to college football was strong, I knew that sticking it out and helping the kids was my first priority.

What if I decided not to become vulnerable? Sometimes we forget that God has orchestrated these moves for a reason. There wasn't anything I did wrong to land in the spot I landed in. God wanted me to take the focus off of the destination a.k.a. "end goal" and put my faith in Him. He wanted me to become vulnerable so He could use me to fulfill His purposes. I was rewarded in December of 2013 and 2014 for being vulnerable to those players in that school district. We won back-to-back state championships and the lessons I learned proved to be the most fruitful for my career growth.

In times where you may not always feel like you're in the place you want to be, remember that God's grace is more than sufficient to help you endure and help you get what you need while in your moment. Remember this scripture: Hebrews 4:16: *"Let us therefore come boldly unto the throne of grace, that we may obtain mercy, and find grace to help in time of need."* Your vulnerability allows God to do His work in you by you dropping your guard. Becoming vulnerable simply allows everyone around you to share in the successes God has put in you. Adding value to the coaches and players you're around makes the program better, but more importantly God's program, agenda, and plan for you is put to work. Don't place God on pause. Open up, be used, and pour into your position group no matter the stop on your coaching journey. Remember as I had to, He's placing you strategically in these positions to do His work.

Pre-Season Week 1 to Week 4 Daily Coaches Daily Life Management Plan

In 2017, I initially served as an Offensive Intern for the Cleveland Browns. I was an assistant coach to the Quarterbacks Coach David Lee, serving him in whatever capacity he needed to do his job better. If that was film breakdown, specifically opponent coverages for the pre-season or regular season games, I did it. If it was gathering information for the opponents defense with regards to fronts, stunts, or personnel, I

provided that information and formulated it in the Offensive Scouting notebook for our weekly game plan.

As I progressed through the OTAs (Organized Team Activities) in the spring, the opportunity to continue as a member of the staff was becoming more apparent due to a coach leaving the staff. When I returned for training camp, God opened a door for me. He covered me and provided me an opportunity for growth at the highest level of football. In every position on a coaching staff there's a place to be a servant for God, but when you're a Quality Control Coach/Assistant position coach, your time, effort, and detail in the information you provide must be accurate, measured, and timely because everything you do is depended on. In this role, I had to master my organizational skills like no other time in my coaching career. My previous college experiences only partially prepared me for this particular position.

I had to be adept at serving the position coach and the players simultaneously. Quite honestly, it was the best job I've ever had as a coach because I knew that God had planted me firmly in that spot. Whether you're a position coach, an assistant to an assistant, a Quality Control Coach, the Coordinator, or the Head Coach, it's imperative to consider the following as you prepare for the regular season. This is the time to test your organizational strategy with how you'll spend your time with God when the real bullets begin to fly in a few weeks.

Let's begin!

Day 1 - The Postmortem Meeting with the Team

I've learned over time, especially in marriage, to think before I speak. So I encourage you to pray before you text, talk on the phone, or confront your players after an emotionally draining game. As a player, I've experienced the backlash and frustration from a coach still reliving the heartbreaking loss, and as a younger coach, I recall the memories of still living in the previous Saturday's loss and making the players relive it to. It's time turn the page and look forward to the next battle and a solution. If it was a win from the previous week, it's time to move forward into a new week so you don't stay too long in the past. Regardless, it's important to seek God for clarity of thought so you can move forward.

Scripture Reminder

Proverbs 3:5-6

5 Trust in the Lord with all your heart; do not depend on your own understanding.

6 Seek his will in all you do, and he will show you which path to take.

Day 2 - The Game Planning Meeting with the Coaches

This can be a long and painful meeting, but it also can be a highly productive meeting depending on the relationships between you and the other coaches on your side of the ball. This is the critical buy-in meeting of the week. Pray and ask God to give you an open heart and open mind to work hand-in-hand with your peers to have the best game plan for the players, not the best plan for your ego.

Scripture Reminder

John 3:30

He must become greater and greater, and I must become less and less.

Day 3 - The Scouting Report Meeting with the Players:

At this point, you've bought in and you believe in what the game plan is for the next opponent. Go in with the right body language so the players can see that you not only believe in what the coaches have put together, but you believe in the team enough to know that this is the way forward. The battle lines are marked now; let's go practice the strategy. Anything less than what I conveyed is so counterproductive that it destroys the continuity of the entire team. This is always the reason for prayer.

Scripture Reminder

1 Peter 3:8

8 Finally, all of you should be of one mind. Sympathize with each other. Love each other as brothers and sisters. Be tenderhearted, and keep a humble attitude.

Day 4-5 - The Position Group Prayer:
Whether it's post practice or pre-practice, encourage your group to huddle up and pray about the task at hand for the day. Prayer is a great grounder and settler for the spirit. It allows your players to understand more intimately, who is in charge and who they are depending on. As a veteran coach of 25 years, I encourage my position group to start practice with prayer before everyone gets on the field. As we near game day, the constant prayer keeps the group centered and the trust of the game in God's hands. There's only adjustments once we're past the kickoff!

Scripture Reminder

1 Corinthians 1:10
10 I appeal to you, dear brothers and sisters, by the authority of our Lord Jesus Christ, to live in harmony with each other. Let there be no divisions in the church. Rather, be of one mind, united in thought and purpose.

Game Day Pre-Game:
Duplicate what you've practiced all week, keep a steady hand and keep faith in what you've asked God for. Don't look for ulterior game plans. Trust what you've given your men. Anything less than that is called panicking. You are not built to panic, only to trust in the God you've called upon all this time.

Scripture Reminder

Proverbs 24:10
If you fail under pressure, your strength is too small.

Game Day Post Game:

An old coach that I used to work for would say to me after a game, "Coach, it's not as good as it seems, but it's not as bad as it seems either. Let's go back and look at the film!" Even if you saw something problematic and it annoys you, keep your calm and show a steady hand when you hit that locker room door. Remember this, your players will remember the short fuse that you had.

The Proverbs 24:10 scripture holds true here because you want to carry your position group into the next week knowing that you are prepared to make things better. The worst time to coach them up is at a post-game press conference or meeting. Review the film, thank God for coming away healthy and for the victory or for the lessons learned in defeat. It's all about preserving your perspective and righteous mind for the next week.

Scripture Reminder

Proverbs 24:10

If you fail under pressure, your strength is too small.

Plan God into your work! Schedule Planning:

Before you go on to the regular season, document your weekly schedule and your time with God. Some tasks that you've taken on require so much patience and that time with Him before the tasks are completed is vital. Please take the time to plan your week. The organization will go a long way in helping you map out your week. From walks, lunches or working out, this chart can be something that helps you engage the spiritual man weekly and be used as a measure of accountability for you.

God Time	Monday	Tuesday	Wednesday	Thursday	Friday	Saturday	Sunday

The Season

Season Week 1
Just Execute...No Over Thinking...Just Trust

After weeks of practicing, grinding, sweating, toiling and pushing through the mundane, you should be at a point of achieving some muscle memory in the players' execution in all three phases of the game (offense, defense, and special teams). The audition is over, the roster is set in place, the "hay's in the barn," as some of my old fellow Texas coaches would say, and the game is finally here. No more waiting.

How much of this are you going to give to God? Are you confident that He has your back with reference to the preparation? That's always the most important aspect of preparation. Are you going to be even keeled or are you going to take over and just call on God at the pre-game prayer, then call Him again on the post-game prayer whether you win or lose? If you had a rough season last year, do you dwell on that?

Look, simply put, if God is running this process for you, you have to trust Him. This may be the make or break season with regards to a contract extension and you keeping your job. No matter what's on the line, it's not tougher than God's will and way for you. Don't add ingredients to the already huge pot that's cooking on the stove.

There's nothing greater than using football and our lengthy and orderly preparation as a microcosm of life. We have pressures, stresses, doubts, and fears but if we reflect long enough, we have to remember who we're asking to be in charge. If the person in charge is not you, may I offer a suggestion as you head into this first week of eventful competition that counts in the win-loss column.

Scripture

Joshua 1:9
This is my command – be strong and courageous! Do not be afraid or discouraged. For the Lord your God is with you wherever you go.

God called on Joshua after Moses' death to go forth into the land God had for His people. Imagine Joshua's nerves at that moment. Imagine your back-up quarterback taking over early in the game when he's only been getting 20% of the reps as part of his preparation. What makes this command of God so powerful is He already knows what He's doing. The land is already prepped for His people, He chose Joshua to go forth into it and be courageous.

Coaches, God is not taking you into a foreign land with a rifle and a unit of soldiers. He's preparing you for another battle to be played out on a football field. I'm not saying the journey this week isn't significant, but please keep in perspective that the result of your Friday night, Saturday afternoon, or Sunday game is dependent on who you're putting first and who's in the lead position. Remember one of your reminders, The "Old Iso" Play (Who's Leading?).

Let's go Coach! Focus on the mission of Joshua.

Prayer

Heavenly Father, provide me the peace to relax this week. Strengthen me to exude enthusiasm, not stress or strain, rather faith in You that I'm listening clearly to Your entire game plan as I proceed into this week. In Jesus Name. Amen.

Thought process for the week:

As you head into the first week of the season, you've taken some time to evaluate your schedule, routine, coaches, and players. Are you okay?

Have you taken some time to put God into the daily rhythm of the season?

Where is He with regards to the weekly routine as it involves practice planning and game planning?

Reminders:

How are you in these areas this week? Please take some time to journal on your reminders this week.

1) Power of Words. How were you this week with yours?

____

____

____

2) The Old Iso Play…Who's leading? Man, who's running the show this week? Where are you with that?

____

____

____

3) Don't Worry About Vulnerability. Did you give somebody a portion of you this week? Where are you with that?

____

____

____

Remember:

1) Day 1, pray before the staff game planning meeting. Remove yourself and fill God in.

2) Day 2, pray before the scouting report meeting with the team. See Reminders!

3) Day 3, pray before meeting with position group. See Reminders!

4) Day 4-5, pray with position group for the remainder of the week to help you and the guys remain grounded. If it's about Him, make it about Him in all areas. Not just sometimes. This is a great way to start practice.

Season Week 2
Establishing Trust

Establishing trust, two very powerful words. It is essential in any relationship you deem to be significant. As you lay your head down the night before your game this weekend, ask yourself, "Have I created a bond, established trust, and made a connection with these men?"

More than likely you've already accomplished this and it's a result of the success you've had. As you spend time daily laying the foundation with your players, driving out of them the essential principles they need to be successful as men on and off the field, remember God is working to do the same thing in you.

He is constantly working to gain your trust. Through every adversity, God wants you to look up and know He is there extending His hand to you. Every time you get a little frustrated with the "game script" of life and begin to think it's too hard and simply not working, think of how masterful God has coached you up and prepared you. Think on how He has established trust within you. Having the Lord leading you daily and you not wanting to let Him down should correlate to your players not wanting to let you down. It's the relationship that produces this passion. Always remember just how important it is to establish that trust because God shapes you daily to do the exact same thing so we can execute His plan better.

Scripture

Isaiah 26:4
Trust ye in the Lord for ever: for in the Lord Jehovah is everlasting strength.

Prayer

As we go forward this weekend into the most important game on the schedule... the next game, help us to trust You for wisdom. Let us not lean on our own understanding, but trust in You for everything. Help us to develop our players, build trust, and do things as You've led us to do with these men daily. Give us a sharp ear to hear Your voice and

execute what You put on our hearts and not waver in the process. In Jesus Name. Amen.

Thought process for the week:

As you head into Week 2 of the season, have you taken some time to evaluate your schedule, routine, coaches and players. Are you okay?

Have you taken some time to put God into the daily rhythm of the season?

Where is He with regards to the weekly routine as it involves practice planning and game planning?

Reminders:

How are you in these areas this week? Please take some time to journal on your reminders this week.

1) Power of Words. How were you this week with yours?

____

____

____

2) The Old Iso Play…Who's leading? Man, who's running the show this week? Where are you with that?

____

____

____

3) Don't Worry About Vulnerability. Did you give somebody a portion of you this week? Where are you with that?

____

____

____

Remember:

1) Day 1, pray before the staff game planning meeting. Remove yourself and fill God in.

2) Day 2, pray before the scouting report meeting with the team. See Reminders!

3) Day 3, pray before meeting with position group. See Reminders!

4) Day 4-5, pray with position group for the remainder of the week to help you and the guys remain grounded. If it's about Him, make it about Him in all areas. Not just sometimes. This is a great way to start practice.

Season Week 3
Urgency and Expectation

The posture of a great fighter is always one that displays a stance of him ready to throw punches and defend himself. He may not always be accurate but he's ready to "pop" his hands, throw a jab, throw a hook, throw a body shot, or defend himself. His hands are never down; he always has a focus and he's looking at what's coming.

That essentially is the definition of urgency and expectation. He's prepared to receive based on what he's producing! He's putting in work, he has an alertness, a hypersensitivity to his surroundings. He's focused on all that's in front of him. He's not distracted with the crowd, the lights and the voices around him. There's only one voice that matters to him and that is his corner-man! He's managed to cut out all the distractions and hone in on that one voice for his direction. Once he's been given his assignment, he executes the plan with a "life on the line" urgency and as a result, he's awaiting a mighty blessing in return. This is his expectation.

This weekend, as you tune into improvement and building your men, concentrate on doing all God has guided you to do with a level of urgency not laziness. Your corner-man, God, has supplied you with instructions. Cut out the noise around you and the opinions of those that really don't matter and stand bold. Be confident about the direction God has led you into and always expect the best outcome. Remember today (and teach as often as possible), urgency and expectation in all you do.

Scripture

Romans 13:11
This is all the more urgent, for you know how late it is; time is running out. Wake up, for our salvation is nearer now than when we first believed.

Prayer

Heavenly Father, help me to stay focused on you. Give me the posture of a great fighter ready and willing at all times to serve You. Strengthen me daily to stay alert, focused, and ready. In Jesus Name. Amen.

Thought process for the week:

As you head into Week 3 of the season, have you taken some time to evaluate your schedule, routine, coaches, and players. Are you okay?

Have you taken some time to put God into the daily rhythm of the season?

Where is He with regards to the weekly routine as it involves practice planning and game planning?

Reminders:

How are you in these areas this week?

Please take some time to journal on your reminders this week.

1) Power of Words. How were you this week with yours?

____

____

____

2) The Old Iso Play…Who's leading? Man, who's running the show this week? Where are you with that?

____

____

____

3) Don't Worry About Vulnerability. Did you give somebody a portion of you this week? Where are you with that?

____

____

____

Remember:

1) Day 1, pray before the staff game planning meeting. Remove yourself and fill God in.

2) Day 2, pray before the scouting report meeting with the team. See Reminders!

3) Day 3, pray before meeting with position group. See Reminders!

4) Day 4-5, pray with position group for the remainder of the week to help you and the guys remain grounded. If it's about Him, make it about Him in all areas. Not just sometimes. This is a great way to start practice.

Season Week 4
Values vs Feelings

What defines you? Let me rephrase it. What is at the core of what you believe? Whatever defines you influences and affects how you coach and how you build your team or your position group. There is no fence walking; who you are is who you are. What you are when you're away from the facility is what you are in front of your players, it is the essence of your character. You may not always see it but the players see it.

Have you ever seen your players mock or mimic you? Most of the time, they are right on point because they model what they see daily from you. Here's what we have to remember:

Value
Opportunities while being
Consistent with your
Attitude and
Leadership

Brothers be vocal! God has already given you a Word, He's put it right at your core. True coaching success comes from you teaching what God's put inside you. It'll never come out unless you open your mouth. If you **V**alue **O**pportunities while being **C**onsistent with your **A**ttitude and **L**eadership, you're going to be successful in this profession. You're either going to be in control or allow God to drive. When you allow God to drive, your values bloom. When you strive to keep your values at the forefront of developing your men, you don't allow your feelings to take control. You're too busy executing God's game plan. Your feelings cause you to lose control and when you do, you begin to leak like a car leaking oil. Things come out that otherwise shouldn't come out. When you stand on your values, your players will follow. Much like developing your family at home, you stand on a set of values for your children. No matter the difficulty, stick with your God given values and be vocal! Listen and execute God's plan daily and avoid the feelings of not executing His script because it seems too difficult. There's success waiting for those that can hang in there and trust God's plan!

Scripture

Ephesians 1:4-5

4 Even before he made the world, God loved us and chose us in Christ to be holy and without fault in his eyes.
5 God decided in advance to adopt us into his own family by bringing us to himself through Jesus Christ. This is what he wanted to do, and it gave him great pleasure.

Prayer

Father God, help me to stay the course You've put me on. Sometimes the challenges are great, teach me daily how to stand bold and listen and execute Your game plan with our players. Strengthen me not to leak by getting caught up in my feelings. Teach me daily how to stand on the values You've put inside me. In Jesus Name. Amen.

Thought process for the week:

As you head into Week 4 of the season, have you taken some time to evaluate your schedule, routine, coaches, and players. Are you okay?

Have you taken some time to put God into the daily rhythm of the season?

Where is He with regards to the weekly routine as it involves practice planning and game planning?

Reminders:

How are you in these areas this week? Please take some time to journal on your reminders this week.

1) Power of Words. How were you this week with yours?

____

____

____

2) The Old Iso Play…Who's leading? Man, who's running the show this week? Where are you with that?

____

____

____

3) Don't Worry About Vulnerability. Did you give somebody a portion of you this week? Where are you with that?

____

____

____

Remember:

1) Day 1, pray before the staff game planning meeting. Remove yourself and fill God in.

2) Day 2, pray before the scouting report meeting with the team. See Reminders!

3) Day 3, pray before meeting with position group. See Reminders!

4) Day 4-5, pray with position group for the remainder of the week to help you and the guys remain grounded. If it's about Him, make it about Him in all areas. Not just sometimes. This is a great way to start practice.

2nd Quarter of Season Self-Assessment
"A Walk with God"

The life of an NFL Quality Control coach is an unending world between Thursday and Tuesday. Getting ahead of the curve with your breakdown assignments for upcoming opponents is vital. In order to maximize your time, you have to have a system of checks and balances, a schedule, and coffee often. As Coach Kirby Wilson, a mentor of mine in Cleveland used to always tell me, "John, you got to break down the breakdown." Wilson is a lifelong NFL Running Back Coach and Run Game Coordinator who spent time in a few NFL organizations. He understood what success looked like having been a part of several Super Bowl appearances and victories.

I remember the first time I sat down with Coach Wilson in Cleveland, "JT, I need you to stop by my office every day, even if it's only for five minutes. If that's all we have during the day, make sure you visit with me so we can talk." This coach indeed poured into my life and always gave me perspective about this part of my journey. Men like him were rare in my life up to this point, but I've been blessed to have met a few along the way that wanted to educate and elevate young coaches aspiring to grow. He would always tell me to stay ahead of the tidal waves of chaos by managing my work daily.

Now Coach Wilson was detailed in how he viewed an opponent and reviewed film, and I strongly took his advice and instructions to heart on the football preparation of analyzing opponents. But I also observed how he made his world so detailed before the football analysis for him ever began. When I would pull up to the facility at 5:15 a.m. every morning, I'd see Coach Wilson's car already at the facility. Later, when I'd go out to set up the indoor field for the QBs who were coming in to throw with the QB Coach, I'd see Coach Wilson going for his morning walk. He told me that this reflection period was part of his routine.

Taking mental notes as I often did, I started to understand over time that to manage my time I needed to "control the controllables" and maintain the things that I thought were important. In order to do that, I needed to schedule what I thought was important in my life to avoid extreme meltdowns and overload. With the schedule of work I had every week, I decided to bring back my walks with God. Back in Dallas, I called it my vision

walk. My wife and I would do it early in the mornings on the weekends. During the work week, we'd do it in the evenings. It was our routine and time to talk.

In Cleveland, I would put on my headphones three to four days a week, including game day, and walk the perimeter of the field listening to whatever artist got me going. The time was priceless and it allowed me to have a moment to reflect with God. Taking that pause and time with God and preparing for my day proved to be fruitful. No matter the circumstances that were about to confront me upstairs in that coaches' meeting room or my desk, I was prepared.

Consider a walk with God even if only for 30 minutes. Between praying while you walk and the gratitude you feel that you get to coach and change lives, it is the best way to start a day as a coach. Start your day Coach! Control the controllables... yourself. Go get the running shoes on, let's go!

Ephesians 4:22-23

22 throw off your old sinful nature and your former way of life, which is corrupted by lust and deception.
23 Instead, let the Spirit renew your thoughts and attitudes.

Season Week 5
Consume the Solution

So what's the approach? You all have issues that you're dealing with when building the team – from chemistry to finding the best men to run the scheme you've put in place. Sometimes, you can find a million things to be frustrated about or simply complain about. From every angle there seems to be a problem. At times, you get so punch drunk from all the blows the problems deliver you, you end up walking around on autopilot. It's almost as if you've checked out emotionally. You're physically there but your mind is not. The great R&B group, The O'Jays said it best, "Your body's here with me but your mind is on the other side of town." Let's address how to get back on track. Let's start with burying the issues. Let's unpack all of our challenges. Let's not make the mountain of problems any larger.

Let's start today by consuming the solution! Don't use the compound effect by adding more concerns to your plate. Thank God first for handling your issues even when you can't see the solution. Second, consume the solution. Be excited about creating a new normal and being an agent of change! The more time we spend on solving the problems instead of carrying out what's wrong in our conversation, the less weight we'll feel. We will then become more mission oriented looking for ways to improve.

God said He wants our burdens so let's give them over to Him and focus on the ability to hear from the Lord and win our trials with solutions that align with Him.

Scripture

Philippians 4:6-8
6 Don't worry about anything; instead, pray about everything. Tell God what you need, and thank him for all he has done.
7 Then you will experience God's peace, which exceeds anything we can understand. His peace will guard your hearts and minds as you live in Christ Jesus.
8 And now, dear brothers and sisters, one final thing. Fix your thoughts on what is true, and honorable, and right, and pure, and lovely, and admirable. Think about things that are excellent and worthy of praise."

Prayer

Heavenly Father, thank You for showing me how to be a problem solver not a problem watcher. Give me great ears, Lord to always hear distinctly from You and act according to Your plan. In Jesus Name. Amen.

Thought process for the week:

As you head into Week 5 of the season, have you taken some time to evaluate your schedule, routine, coaches, and players. Are you okay?

Have you taken some time to put God into the daily rhythm of the season?

Where is He with regards to the weekly routine as it involves practice planning and game planning?

Reminders:

How are you in these areas this week? Please take some time to journal on your reminders this week.

1) Power of Words. How were you this week with yours?

____

____

____

2) The Old Iso Play…Who's leading? Man, who's running the show this week? Where are you with that?

____

____

____

3) Don't Worry About Vulnerability. Did you give somebody a portion of you this week? Where are you with that?

____

____

____

Remember:

1) Day 1, pray before the staff game planning meeting. Remove yourself and fill God in.

2) Day 2, pray before the scouting report meeting with the team. See Reminders!

3) Day 3, pray before meeting with position group. See Reminders!

4) Day 4-5, pray with position group for the remainder of the week to help you and the guys remain grounded. If it's about Him, make it about Him in all areas. Not just sometimes. This is a great way to start practice.

Season Week 6
Don't Press...Stand, Stand Tall

"Chaos is sometimes an unknown friend of breakthrough and it just doesn't know it. Even though things seem rough, hang on, ride it out!"

Chaos, high-volume production, or constant change is not a bad thing when you're thrown into a new situation requiring or calling for your leadership. All three things are instruments on your training ground. They're like dumbbells needed to make you stronger and more prepared for the leadership that's to come.

When under the rigors of this chaos, don't stress and more importantly don't press! A great friend and coach, Ricky Thomas, formerly of the Indianapolis Colts gave me two words years ago that made me look at chaos differently, he simply said, "Don't press." Look to God for direction. He's teaching you first how to handle the situation before you respond to it.

The three things to remember when confronted with chaos is to Pray, Stand, and Expect. Learning how to implement all three will teach you how to stand tall when confronted with pressure and not react or press into an emotional decision on something. Reacting your way and executing God's way are worlds apart.

Let's always remember to Pray, Stand, and Expect. Believe it or not, it's a good plan long before the week's big game. The players will begin to follow the same method of attack because they are watching you stand tall under massive scrutiny, chaos and pressure. Stand Bold!

Scripture

1 Samuel 12:16

"Now therefore stand and see this great thing, which the Lord will do before your eyes."

Prayer

Heavenly Father, thank You for the chaos around me. Continue to show me how to respond Your way. In Jesus Name. Amen.

Thought process for the week:

As you head into Week 6 of the season, have you've taken some time to evaluate your schedule, routine, coaches, and players. Are you okay?

Have you taken some time to put God into the daily rhythm of the season?

Where is He with regards to the weekly routine as it involves practice planning and game planning?

Reminders:

How are you in these areas this week? Please take some time to journal on your reminders this week.

1) Power of Words. How were you this week with yours?

____

____

____

2) The Old Iso Play…Who's leading? Man, who's running the show this week? Where are you with that?

____

____

____

3) Don't Worry About Vulnerability. Did you give somebody a portion of you this week? Where are you with that?

____

____

____

Remember:

1) Day 1, pray before the staff game planning meeting. Remove yourself and fill God in.

2) Day 2, pray before the scouting report meeting with the team. See Reminders!

3) Day 3, pray before meeting with position group. See Reminders!

4) Day 4-5, pray with position group for the remainder of the week to help you and the guys remain grounded. If it's about Him, make it about Him in all areas. Not just sometimes. This is a great way to start practice.

Season Week 7
Compartmentalize

Where does the pain go? Sometimes we get so wrapped up in our craft, there has to be a place to dump all the things we deal with outside of the game. For as long as I can remember, I saw one very strong man. He was my dad. Now at first glance, I thought there was nobody tougher. This man raised me from the tender age of 2 years old by himself. After his death, I realized how he lacked confidence but he shunned his pain and pride to raise a man. He shielded me from a broken home the best he could.

As a young man, all I was familiar with was an old Marine that only had one way of doing things. The emptiness of lacking a mother at home was a burden for a period in life. Here were some of my piled on feelings:

- Meeting my mother when I was 18 and within two months of my first meeting, she left again. She changed her address and telephone number with no warning.
- Later meeting her at 32 years old and her saying, in front of my new wife, that she had to erase me from her life.
- Raising two lovely young daughters on my own, just like my father raised me, for a season in my life before I remarried.

During these moments mentioned, I believe I felt some of what my father may have felt. Rejection, emptiness, lack of confidence, while wondering all the while was it something about myself that caused all of this. I wasn't in a good place, but I reminisced on my childhood and my father's lack of peace at times. I didn't want that for my life. I wanted a resolution, some peace, and a new way forward.

In the span of a few months, between pain and starting over, I learned to compartmentalize the emotions to avoid the weight of the pain. I learned that satan had his own tricks and built-in game plan for those of us struggling with past pain. The last thing God wants is for you to tack on one failure, pain, heartache, and loss with another one. He wants you to give all of it to Him. Not one thing, but all of it. He does not want you to burden yourself with the feelings of emptiness or shortcoming. In the span of time when I learned how to compartmentalize my failures and not pile them on, I

learned what God's true mission for my life was. The danger you all may be experiencing is covering one wound with something that makes you feel good but isn't good for you while never treating the issue. God does not want you to fall for tricks, schemes, and plots that satan has cleverly put in place to wipe you out. Do not fall for the "banana in the tailpipe," as Eddie Murphy said in the movie *Beverly Hills Cop*.

When I was in the NFL, I spent an entire season submerging myself in my work so I didn't have to take on the emotions that I had about losing my dad. It wasn't until around six months, after I returned home and had some much needed quiet time to process all of my emotions, that I felt as if I was starting to truly pick up the pieces from losing him.

There's a powerful scripture that helps remove these feelings of weightiness and burden. Let's consider this, if God had a purpose for you before you were born, why would He press these counterproductive feelings of lack in your life? God is not that type of God. Remember this week to not let the pain of past failures seep into the growth plan God has set out for you.

Scripture

Jeremiah 1:5

I knew you before I formed you in your mother's womb. Before you were born I set you apart and appointed you as my prophet to the nations.

Prayer

Lord, since You got me, help me to not put junk on myself that You've already removed. In Jesus Name. Amen.

Thought process for the week:

As you head into Week 7 of the season, have you taken some time to evaluate your schedule, routine, coaches, and players. Are you okay?

Have you taken some time to put God into the daily rhythm of the season?

Where is He with regards to the weekly routine as it involves practice planning and game planning?

Reminders:

How are you in these areas this week? Please take some time to journal on your reminders this week.

1) Power of Words. How were you this week with yours?

____

____

____

2) The Old Iso Play…Who's leading? Man, who's running the show this week? Where are you with that?

____

____

____

3) Don't Worry About Vulnerability. Did you give somebody a portion of you this week? Where are you with that?

____

____

____

Remember:

1) Day 1, pray before the staff game planning meeting. Remove yourself and fill God in.

2) Day 2, pray before the scouting report meeting with the team. See Reminders!

3) Day 3, pray before meeting with position group. See Reminders!

4) Day 4-5, pray with position group for the remainder of the week to help you and the guys remain grounded. If it's about Him, make it about Him in all areas. Not just sometimes. This is a great way to start practice.

Season Week 8
Keep your head on a swivel!

The title alone makes many of us remember the buzz words we use daily in coaching our players. For the last 25 years, I've heard linebacker coaches yell the term in practice and in drills, but I've snatched the term as well for coaching quarterbacks. Two of the most important positions on the field – besides the offensive and defensive lines – are quarterbacks and linebackers, especially the middle linebacker. They're pitted in the middle of all the chaos for 4-7 second bursts of high energy with a single goal in mind. Their singular decision can most likely dictate the outcome of the play.

With all that's around them, they have to have a hyper-awareness, alertness, or sensitivity to their environment and factor in all they can before the ball is snapped. They do not have time for distraction and focus is a premium!

Imagine God being your head coach and you're His chosen quarterback or middle linebacker and He calls you into His office to speak with you about your assignment. He'd probably say to you, "son, keep your head on a swivel." There's a lot going on around you, life is fast paced and things are moving quickly, but in order for you to be positioned for the life you desire and, more importantly, the life He wants for you, you must "keep your head on a swivel." I have a desire to move further in my own career and develop great men at the highest level of football, but in order for that to happen, I have to "keep my head on a swivel," by staying alert daily, working while I wait, improving in my current position, and trusting God by doing the most with the resources I have.

Brothers, "keep your head on a swivel!" Stay focused and finish the assignment He's assigned you to do.

Scripture

1 Peter 5:8

Be alert and of sober mind. Your enemy the devil prowls around like a roaring lion looking for someone to devour.

Prayer

Lord, thank You for the plan. Help me daily to stay the course that You've set for me. Strengthen me to stay focused through the grind and condition me to handle it better. Whatever I need to go where You're taking me, give me the "swivel" mentality to be sharp and alert. In Jesus Name. Amen.

Thought process for the week:

As you head into Week 8 of the season, have you taken some time to evaluate your schedule, routine, coaches, and players. Are you okay?
Have you taken some time to put God into the daily rhythm of the season?

Where is He with regards to the weekly routine as it involves practice planning and game planning?

Reminders:

How are you in these areas this week? Please take some time to journal on your reminders this week.

1) Power of Words. How were you this week with yours?

____

____

____

2) The Old Iso Play…Who's leading? Man, who's running the show this week? Where are you with that?

____

____

____

3) Don't Worry About Vulnerability. Did you give somebody a portion of you this week? Where are you with that?

____

____

____

Remember:

1) Day 1, pray before the staff game planning meeting. Remove yourself and fill God in.

2) Day 2, pray before the scouting report meeting with the team. See Reminders!

3) Day 3, pray before meeting with position group. See Reminders!

4) Day 4-5, pray with position group for the remainder of the week to help you and the guys remain grounded. If it's about Him, make it about Him in all areas. Not just sometimes. This is a great way to start practice.

Midway Point of Season Self-Assessment
"Uncommon Change, Uncomfortable Commitment"
Bye Week Reflection

In 2010, I began developing a lifelong friendship with Daron Roberts. Daron and I are cut from the same cloth with regards to having a hunger and thirst to pursue a vision. Daron is currently a professor at the University of Texas and is the founding director of the Center for Sports Leadership & Innovation.

Years ago, Daron was an Assistant Defensive Backs Coach and Quality Control Coach for the Cleveland Browns and began his journey with the Kansas City Chiefs. He later became the DB Coach at West Virginia University and has since written multiple books about his journey. "Call An Audible" was one of his most recent books, where he talks about pursuing a vision. I've known Daron for almost 10 years and have watched his growth and how he's impacted people all over the world. We connect a few times a month to check on each other and have a summit of the minds every July at a camp called 4th and 1, developed by Daron more than 10 years ago. The camp serves young men who aspire to play football at the next level. This camp is set up as a life skills, academic development, football skills, and networking camp.

Upon first look, most of the young men think they are coming into this camp to get a star ranking but upon check-in the kids are required to take the ACT and for the next week are trained every day after football practice and lunch in an academic setting that rivals college life. Every day, the skills development flips to another topic whether it's social media behavior, how to manage a checkbook, interviewing skills, or dinner etiquette. We build these young men as if they were NFL draftees heading to the Rookie Symposium. Daron has allowed me to be the head football coach for the football portion of the camp and every year I speak with the campers on "Uncommon Change, Uncomfortable Commitment."

Coaches, as I reflect on the challenges you all face at this moment in the season, it's always critical to remember why you love and do what you do. Beyond the walks in the morning or the organizational skills you have to master, it's important to remember what

keeps you in the profession. Three years ago, I walked into a classroom at Northeast Technical Community College and spoke to the 4th & 1 Campers about how important it was to be uncommon and at the same time uncomfortable with your quest to make an entry into college athletics. As was the case with the 4th and 1 Campers and their quest to play college ball, many coaches – like myself – have aspirations to coach a lifetime in this profession, as well as grow. The road that takes you to where you want to go will differ and you have to be okay with that. Sometimes, where you fail is comparing your process to someone else's, but you have to stay focused on your course.

What do I mean by "Uncommon Change?"

1 Corinthians 10:12-13

12 If you think you are standing strong, be careful not to fall.

13 The temptations in your life are no different from what others experience. And God is faithful. He will not allow the temptation to be more than you can stand. When you are tempted, he will show you a way out so that you can endure.

With the pitfalls and snares that surround you in this profession, and the distractions that you sometimes face or put on yourselves, you have to remain resolute. Although hard at times, depending on what surrounds you, I'm reminded that in order to make a huge dream possible, you have to be set apart, different, and okay with it. This is the "uncommon change" factor I'm talking about. God set you apart for a purpose and everyone is not going to walk on that road of choices with you because what He planned for you is simply for you. Some won't understand your discipline or focus.

As someone who has walked away from six-figure corporate jobs to pursue a full-time life in coaching, I saw a long time ago that this was my first challenge in "Uncommon Change." I've gone through bankruptcy, lost income, and bounced back slowly all for the sake of knowing – not just believing, but knowing – that God has a place for me in this profession at the highest level. My introduction to the NFL was brief in my first visit and a little longer during my second stint, however, He has shown me my future by allowing me to see every angle so I can know how to conduct myself when I return.

What do I mean by "Uncomfortable Commitment"?

Most of my life, thus far, has been filled with a consistent level or rejection in the pursuit of landing the right coaching opportunity, but, thanks to God, resilience has been a key trait of mine. I've spent some moments late at night talking to God after receiving "no" from a pending coaching opportunity. I've had my fair share of "no" return phone calls or emails from General Managers or college coaches, but what keeps me pushing forward? God's promise. In today's world of young athletes that are enamored with making the Twitter announcements of the 50th college offer, everyone gets into the mindset of thinking that it's all easy because it looks easy for someone else. Instead of getting caught up in the media craze of announcements and coaching moves, God has had a tendency to whisper in my ear and confirm with me that there's one place for me. I don't have to be wanted by the whole world.

Isaiah 35:8

And an highway shall be there, and a way, and it shall be called The way of holiness; the unclean shall not pass over it; but it shall be for those: the wayfaring men, though fools, shall not err therein.

Quite honestly, the highway you travel will be different, but God has an ordained "way of holiness." As the scripture reference above indicates in Isaiah 35:8, there's a highway God wants you to take and that highway He's putting you on will truly differ from others. As you wait for a specific blessing from God, it's important to understand that the highway He has you on may be difficult in its terrain and route. It also may be one less traveled but it was designed for you. It may also be uncomfortable with reference to your journey but it was planned for you and when you look back on it upon arriving to your destination, you'll understand its benefit.

As I heard in a mid-season talk about fixed and growth mindset by Justin Su'a, a motivational coach in Cleveland, it's about my perspective. God put this seed of purpose inside me so no matter the "nos" I'm confronted with on this road, I press on. Your "Uncomfortable Commitment" has to be a part of you. In this world of meteoric coaching promotions and rapid rises, it's imperative to remember that it's possible your road may be marred by some slowdowns and rejections but it only last for a season in life

and it happens for a reason.

Sometimes it's not that you're doing anything wrong but God is simply saying, "Not yet! Hold tight. I'm going to equip you to deal with this first before I take you to the palace." You have to be okay with being uncomfortable. As I mentioned to the campers years ago, some of the rejection, family brokenness, and childhood experiences are preparation for my palace presence. The same can be said for the difficulties that you have experienced. The pause, delay, and uncomfortable waiting is God readying you to be a conduit to the coach who had the meteoric rise. It's always about being servants first, not about us being served.

As you head into the second half of your season and you're reminded of the sacrifices made so far, remember the importance of being uncommon and uncomfortable.

Season Week 9
Converting on Life's 3rd & 4th Long

- On January 11, 2004, the Philadelphia Eagles converted a 4th & 26 with a perfectly thrown pass from Donovan McNabb to Freddie Mitchell to keep their playoff hopes alive. The play extended the drive and later gave them a victory.

- On November 16, 2013, the Auburn Tigers converted a 4th & 18 with a huge throw down the middle of the field from Nick Marshall to Ricardo Louis for a 73-yard, game-winning touchdown pass that was tipped by a defender in the process.

- On October 18, 2014, the Notre Dame Fighting Irish converted a 4th & 18, with a timely throw from Everett Golson to Corey Robinson, to keep a drive alive and give their team a shot to pull off a huge win against Florida State.

I could go on all day; the list goes on and on. There's something to be said about each team that was confronted with the challenge of converting on 4th & long. The task always looked difficult, but so is life. Even between these white lines we look so forward to being on, you can't stand up to a task without faith! There's no going "all in" without believing. What's the purpose in you coaching if you don't believe in who you are coaching? Do you seriously think your players can't recognize when you don't believe? From the Sunday scouting breakdown, to the time you hit the field on Friday, Saturday, or Sunday, you have to believe. You have to seek God to clear your thoughts before the pencil hits the sheet!

In each of the examples above, I believe the players didn't approach it exhibiting fear; they approached it believing in success. If you remember nothing else about stepping up to life's tough tasks remember this:

Your converting life's 3rd & 4th and longs are always about where to place your trust. The greater the calling, the more intense the attacks, the closer you are, the more satan will disrupt and destroy the work you've been set apart to do. Execute despite the opposition, see past it no matter what it looks like to those who serve as your critics. Remember, God gave you the vision.

Before the referee spots the ball for what is deemed as the impossible conversion attempt, believe! Believe that God has equipped you and the team to convert. Have faith that it will work out. Teach your players to come to the line of scrimmage believing it's possible.

Scripture

John 14:12-14

12 Very truly I tell you, whoever believes in me will do the works I have been doing, and they will do even greater things than these, because I am going to the Father.
13 And I will do whatever you ask in my name, so that the Father may be glorified in the Son.
14 You may ask me for anything in my name, and I will do it.

Prayer

Lord, before I was born, You equipped me with everything I needed. Continue to teach me to execute the gifts you put inside of me, no matter the situation, show me how to convert! In Jesus Name. Amen.

Thought process for the week:

As you head into Week 9 of the season, have you taken some time to evaluate your schedule, routine, coaches, and players. Are you okay?

Have you taken some time to put God into the daily rhythm of the season?

Where is He with regards to the weekly routine as it involves practice planning and game planning?

Reminders:

How are you in these areas this week? Please take some time to journal on your reminders this week.

1) Power of Words. How were you this week with yours?

____

____

____

2) The Old Iso Play…Who's leading? Man, who's running the show this week? Where are you with that?

____

____

____

3) Don't Worry About Vulnerability. Did you give somebody a portion of you this week? Where are you with that?

____

____

____

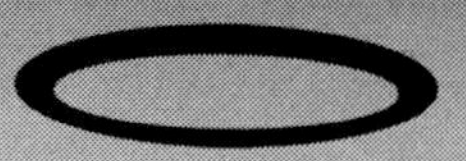

Remember:

1) Day 1, pray before the staff game planning meeting. Remove yourself and fill God in.

2) Day 2, pray before the scouting report meeting with the team. See Reminders!

3) Day 3, pray before meeting with position group. See Reminders!

4) Day 4-5, pray with position group for the remainder of the week to help you and the guys remain grounded. If it's about Him, make it about Him in all areas. Not just sometimes. This is a great way to start practice.

Season Week 10

Beat the man in front of you!

From the first time many of us competed, we had someone tell us, "Be the best!" There's nothing wrong with you striving to be your best, but what exactly does being "The Best" mean? Brother, that's a complicated equation that we don't have all the parts of the formula to solve!

Your legacy, your effort, your early morning grind, and late night studying can't be measured. Your life story, your experiences that humbled you, and adversities that shaped you are unique. Your road to your destiny can't be coupled or compared to someone else's. There's no one on the face of this earth that can define "Your Best!" What I'm trying to say is, there's no comparing your best to anyone else's. You've been set apart not to do good work, but great work.

As you prepare for your late season run, the most obvious objective for you as coaches is to prepare your young men to be their very best by you being your very best daily! You recruited these young men with a purpose in mind. You've endured with them and you understand them. You see glimpses of great promise. Help your players to focus, teach them how to maximize their efforts so they can be what God made them to be, "their very best." If you focus on your best efforts, you end up focusing from inside-out. Your best is what drives the legacy God is defining for you. Coach, this is an individual race you are running.

Compete today with yourself and win! Look yourself in the mirror and say, "You'll never beat me at me being my best." Win the battle within and the outside victory won't be as difficult.

Scripture

Psalms 139:13-15

13 For you created my inmost being; you knit me together in my mother's womb.

14 I praise you because I am fearfully and wonderfully made; your works are wonderful, I know that full well.

15 My frame was not hidden from you when I was made in the secret place, when I was woven together in the depths of the earth.

Prayer

Father, help me to focus daily on competing with myself. I'm the one opponent I know all too well. Let me defeat yesterday's effort with maximum effort today. Teach me how to be my very best for you and those You've allowed me to share this walk with. In Jesus Name, Amen.

Thought process for the week:

As you head into Week 10 of the season, have you taken some time to evaluate your schedule, routine, coaches, and players. Are you okay?

Have you taken some time to put God into the daily rhythm of the season?

Where is He with regards to the weekly routine as it involves practice planning and game planning?

Reminders:

How are you in these areas this week? Please take some time to journal on your reminders this week.

1) Power of Words. How were you this week with yours?

____

____

____

2) The Old Iso Play…Who's leading? Man, who's running the show this week? Where are you with that?

____

____

____

3) Don't Worry About Vulnerability. Did you give somebody a portion of you this week? Where are you with that?

____

____

____

Remember:

1) Day 1, pray before the staff game planning meeting. Remove yourself and fill God in.

2) Day 2, pray before the scouting report meeting with the team. See Reminders!

3) Day 3, pray before meeting with position group. See Reminders!

4) Day 4-5, pray with position group for the remainder of the week to help you and the guys remain grounded. If it's about Him, make it about Him in all areas. Not just sometimes. This is a great way to start practice.

Season Week 11
Mimic Success

In the book of Matthew, Chapter 7, verses 7 and 8 say: *7 "Ask and it will be given to you; seek and you will find; knock and the door will be opened to you. 8 For everyone who asks receives; the one who seeks finds; and to the one who knocks, the door will be opened."*

Amen, that's an awesome Word! Many of us write down the scripture reference on game-day, close the Bible, leave the hotel conference room, the church pew, or the meeting room and begin to line up the list of your desires.

If you scroll down further in Matthew 7 to verses 13-14, it says: *13 "Enter through the narrow gate. For wide is the gate and broad is the road that leads to destruction, and many enter through it. 14 But small is the gate and narrow the road that leads to life, and only a few find it."*

To truly find success in your passion, there's a model. The model is in God's Word. It is your road map and the Holy Spirit is your Corner Man. You must teach your players the same things many of you have come to experience over this life, "the little things," "the extra," "the get-up early," "the go all out," and "the doing more" is required. When you enter the small gate and the narrow road there aren't many there. That's why the road is so narrow because only extraordinary people travel it. It's a tough road that requires more. If you want more, you have to do the extra-ordinary and sometimes travel alone!

Mimicking success is trusting the model that God relays to us in His Word. Look at the life and trials of Jesus Christ. He fulfilled God's Will, fed a multitude of people, prophesied and taught constantly, and sacrificed His life for us. He was the model. He sacrificed for us and was tireless in His efforts. His passion was us! Our passion in this coaching profession is to serve God by serving our players. Whatever you're seeking this season, go all in, follow the model and be willing to walk that narrow road. It's going to require more, but that's the sacrifice for the success you want. Listen to God when He's urging you to do that extra or think out of the box when coaching that drill or diffusing that problem.

Scripture

Matthew 7:13-14

13 Enter through the narrow gate. For wide is the gate and broad is the road that leads to destruction, and many enter through it.
14 But small is the gate and narrow the road that leads to life, and only a few find it.

Prayer

Lord, help me to stay engaged! I know I need to be all ears. Allow me to be all I'm supposed to be for You and as a result, I can be all I'm supposed to be for these men. In Jesus Name. Amen.

Thought process for the week:

As you head into Week 11 of the season, have you taken some time to evaluate your schedule, routine, coaches, and players. Are you okay?

Have you taken some time to put God into the daily rhythm of the season?

Where is He with regards to the weekly routine as it involves practice planning and game planning?

Reminders:

How are you in these areas this week? Please take some time to journal on your reminders this week.

1) Power of Words. How were you this week with yours?

____

____

____

2) The Old Iso Play…Who's leading? Man, who's running the show this week? Where are you with that?

____

____

____

3) Don't Worry About Vulnerability. Did you give somebody a portion of you this week? Where are you with that?

____

____

____

Remember:

1) Day 1, pray before the staff game planning meeting. Remove yourself and fill God in.

2) Day 2, pray before the scouting report meeting with the team. See Reminders!

3) Day 3, pray before meeting with position group. See Reminders!

4) Day 4-5, pray with position group for the remainder of the week to help you and the guys remain grounded. If it's about Him, make it about Him in all areas. Not just sometimes. This is a great way to start practice.

Season Week 12
Awareness

Its 1:45 a.m., and you're working your way to the bathroom. Its pitch black, you can't see your hand in front of you but you have the general direction down to a science. You're moving slowly, carefully, and you can hear each footstep you take because it's so quiet. With the unknown obstacles around you, you're uncomfortable but more than anything, you are aware.

Have you ever started on a job and you're the new guy that doesn't know anyone? You start in your new environment quiet, observant, and in some ways uncomfortable. You want to make a great impression, you want to do good work, and you are seeking growth, so even though your uncomfortable, you are aware! For many, when awareness stops, the three 'Ds' take root:

Disinterested
Disrespectful
Disconnected

Whether it's coaching your players to a Super Bowl, National Championship, or State Championship or for that matter, finishing a great season where a lot of improvement took place and the season was done last week, you have to maintain a level of uncomfortable awareness.

When you're uncomfortable, you maintain a focus as if you're in a dark room seeking the light. You never get too relaxed and you keep the task at hand directly in front of you. In many ways, God aligns your experiences in this same way. He wants us to seek Him and never stray from seeking Him. He wants you to give Him your very best in all you do. He wants you to take the time to call on Him for a guide to plot the course even if you don't have a plan. If you're struggling in your uncomfortableness, He wants you to be aware enough to call Him.

God doesn't want you sticking the ball out and celebrating before you cross the goal line

to your destiny. He doesn't want you being puffed up, thinking that all your success came solely from your own efforts. If you spend the time focusing on the mission cut out for you, you will find that you'll reach higher heights because all you do will be about the destiny and not you. It will be about Him. The uncomfortable awareness He gives you is put in place to make sure you finish the mission cut out for you and to be prepared for the next mission He is shaping.

Scripture

2 Corinthians 12:8-10

8 Three different times I begged the Lord to take it away.
9 Each time he said, "My grace is all you need. My power works best in weakness." So now I am glad to boast about my weaknesses, so that the power of Christ can work through me.
10 That's why I take pleasure in my weaknesses, and in the insults, hardships, persecutions, and troubles that I suffer for Christ. For when I am weak, then I am strong."

Prayer

Father God, I pray for constant awareness in all my uncomfortable situations and, Lord when I'm starting to slip, help me to be uncomfortable enough as if it was the first day on the job. Give me a level of concentration, appreciation, and commitment to do Your work thoroughly in all You put in my hand. In Jesus Name. Amen.

Thought process for the week:

As you head into Week 12 of the season, have you taken some time to evaluate your schedule, routine, coaches, and players. Are you okay?

Have you taken some time to put God into the daily rhythm of the season?

Where is He with regards to the weekly routine as it involves practice planning and game planning?

Reminders:

How are you in these areas this week? Please take some time to journal on your reminders this week.

1) Power of Words. How were you this week with yours?

____

____

____

2) The Old Iso Play…Who's leading? Man, who's running the show this week? Where are you with that?

____

____

____

3) Don't Worry About Vulnerability. Did you give somebody a portion of you this week? Where are you with that?

____

____

____

Remember:

1) Day 1, pray before the staff game planning meeting. Remove yourself and fill God in.

2) Day 2, pray before the scouting report meeting with the team. See Reminders!

3) Day 3, pray before meeting with position group. See Reminders!

4) Day 4-5, pray with position group for the remainder of the week to help you and the guys remain grounded. If it's about Him, make it about Him in all areas. Not just sometimes. This is a great way to start practice.

3rd Quarter of Season Self-Assessment
"Healthy Body & Spirit"

This is what I consider the back-end of the season, coming out of the Thanksgiving holiday and heading into the Christmas season. This is the time that the stress mode changes. There's something about that back quarter of the season where either playoffs – or wondering if you're going to keep your job – all factor into your psyche. Coach, no matter what you're going through right now, please mind your health, body and spirit. There's excitement in knowing that you're going to the playoffs or a major bowl game. Sometimes it gets you out of the routine. Let me encourage you to keep, maintain, and focus on your routine because it was this routine that has helped you get this far. Changing up the grind now sometimes creates an unnecessary panic and it can impact how you eat, sleep, and connect with God.

1 Thessalonians 5:16-18

16 always be joyful.

17 Never stop praying.

18 Be thankful in all circumstances, for this is God's will for you who belong to Christ Jesus."

Let's remember to always keep the shine! The smile, the perspective, and the God character. Don't shun the routine now because circumstances have changed. If your season is in worse condition and you're not sure you'll make it to the next contract, hang on! Remember to always be joyful. God will make a way. Don't let the stresses of what's around you impact the table of physical eating or your lack of time spent with God daily in prayer and talking to Him. Coach, stay connected.

Now over the years, I have lost some hair and when I departed my last job I recognized I may have lost more hair than in years past. The curls of yesterday were replaced with a South American dirt landing strip on the top of my head. The pants didn't fit the same and the repair for me wasn't realized until my postseason walks resumed and I regrouped my eating habits. Sometimes, we find ourselves stress eating or drinking or simply pausing our time with God. Remind yourself to stay engaged and continue to answer God's call like you did when the season began. The consistency is what separates true champions.

Life is to be lived intentionally and that occurs by you first recognizing it and, second, being bold enough to know that we have to remain steady, as you did prior to the shift to the back third of the season. Condition yourself as if you were a boxer in the late 70s and early 80s where they had to take part in 15-round fights. Then, the gloves were heavier and the rings were bigger and there was no place to run. Endurance in that era of boxing was required. Recall the conditioning required early in the season and keep your spiritual man and physical body together no matter the circumstances.

Season Week 13

Run, Walk… Just get there!

Do you remember when you first started coaching? Let me tell you, I was excited, engaged, wide-eyed, on point and asking questions constantly! Whatever the head coach needed from me, I was ALL IN! I was much like a child with a new toy.

But for some of you, the fire dimmed, stuff happened, life changed, distractions of all kinds began to show up – bad women, divorce, unstable home life, your kids' growing pains – and all of a sudden that new job got old real fast. The luster became dull!

Do you remember King David? When David was an awkward looking shepherd boy, he had passion, he wasn't afraid, he took on all challenges and wanted opportunity. God saw something in him that no human could see. When David became king, he encountered numerous distractions. The one that comes to mind immediately, was his lust for a married woman, Bathsheba (Read 2 Samuel 11). He was given a gift and, for a moment, he lost his way on his path of being a great leader.

Brothers, what about you? Let's not allow distractions that you may have created, or someone unjustly thrust into your life, to throttle down your gift and calling to build up these men. Satan will expose you in ways that will ruin the seed that God put inside you if you stay down the road of distractions. The distractions you create are more than just women. They're typically anything that stymies God's intended purpose for you. The love of self, trying to be bigger than God's already bigger plan for you, is usually the starting point of your destruction. I'm sure – from the outside looking in – some of you have seen it all in this profession.

On February 11, 1990, Buster Douglas knocked out Mike Tyson. After that night, the blueprint to beating Mike was put in place. Everyone used the same tactic that Buster Douglas used in pushing Mike into deep waters late into a fight when he'd run out of gas. Brothers, protect your blueprint. Don't let satan expose you so you can't be of value to

God's greater purpose in this profession you love so much. Satan studies your habits. He's your greatest enemy and has a game plan for your failure. Guard yourself by getting in tune with God's game plan daily. Give Him your time in His Word. Run, walk, be still, but get to God and don't go backwards into old habits. Get to Him and stay with Him!

Scripture

Romans 12:2

don't copy the behavior and customs of this world, but let God transform you into a new person by changing the way you think. Then you will learn to know God's will for you, which is good and pleasing and perfect.

Prayer

God, I pray for a renewed spirit and a constant focus on why You blessed me to be in this profession. Teach me, daily, how to keep my love for You in this sport I love being a part of. Let me show up every day as if it's my first day. In Jesus Name. Amen.

Thought process for the week:

As you head into the final phase of the season, take the pulse of your position group, evaluate your schedule, routine, coaches, and players. Are you okay?

Have you taken some time to put God into the daily rhythm of the season?

Where is He with regards to the weekly routine as it involves practice planning and game planning?

Are you ready to shut it down mentally or do you have the strength to finish strong?

Reminders:

How are you in these areas this week? Please take some time to journal on your reminders this week.

1) Power of Words. How were you this week with yours?

____

____

____

2) The Old Iso Play…Who's leading? Man, who's running the show this week? Where are you with that?

____

____

____

3) Don't Worry About Vulnerability. Did you give somebody a portion of you this week? Where are you with that?

____

____

____

Remember:

1) Day 1, pray before the staff game planning meeting. Remove yourself and fill God in.

2) Day 2, pray before the scouting report meeting with the team. See Reminders!

3) Day 3, pray before meeting with position group. See Reminders!

4) Day 4-5, pray with position group for the remainder of the week to help you and the guys remain grounded. If it's about Him, make it about Him in all areas. Not just sometimes. This is a great way to start practice.

Season Week 14

5 loaves, 2 fish! You got all you need!

In the book of Luke, chapter 9, verse 16, it says, *"Jesus took the five loaves and two fish, looked up toward heaven, and blessed them. Then, breaking the loaves into pieces, he kept giving the bread and fish to the disciples so they could distribute it to the people."* Do you know that Jesus fed about 5,000 men, women, and children that day? Wow! The supply appeared low, but He fed the masses and still had some left over.

In Mark 8:6-7 and Matthew 14:16-21, the accounts of Jesus' greatness are similar. In those books it says that it was seven loaves and some small fish but you get the point. He had plenty!

As you approach Week 14, you're either in the midst of a playoff run, finding out who your bowl opponent is, or in reflection mode from the long season you've been fighting through to finish or recently finished. This is considered in many ways, "the dogfight days" of early December. You may have found yourself looking at your personnel and shaking your head in disbelief wondering if something is going to fall out the sky and give you a lift to push through to victory. Some of you may be completely content in this part of your season, but at some point in your career, you've reflected on the need to take your team to another level.

Brothers let me tell you, you've got all you need. To get the trophy and the ring, you've got "5 loaves and 2 fish." You're already equipped for victory! When you review your life and look back on all your days of lack, God put in your hand everything you needed to get through those storms. When you review your team and each player one by one, you may find that some assembly is required! If so, give the necessary time to groom the guys that want to be a part of the future success.

Our profession is indeed a bottom-line business and results driven. Redefining or redesigning your team is a part of building it. You've been given "5 loaves and 2 fish" worth of wisdom to make the decisions necessary to build the best product. The next time you drop your head in frustration or get discouraged at what you have, say to yourself,

"I've got 5 loaves and 2 fish, I got all I need to win." Victory always starts inside you. You represent victory before the ball is ever snapped. It starts with the seed God planted inside of you. Remember, you got all you need and more.

Scripture

Luke 9:13-17

13 But Jesus said, "You feed them." "But we have only five loaves of bread and two fish," they answered. "Or are you expecting us to go and buy enough food for this whole crowd?"
14 For there were about 5,000 men there. Jesus replied, "Tell them to sit down in groups of about fifty each."
15 So the people all sat down.
16 Jesus took the five loaves and two fish, looked up toward heaven, and blessed them. Then, breaking the loaves into pieces, he kept giving the bread and fish to the disciples so they could distribute it to the people.
17 They all ate as much as they wanted, and afterward, the disciples picked up twelve baskets of leftovers!

Prayer

Heavenly Father, help me to always remember that because of You, I was born, bred, conditioned and seasoned to win. Lord, when I start to lose focus on the task You've given me, remind me that, "I've got 5 loaves and 2 fish." In Jesus Name. Amen.

Thought process for the week:

As you head into Week 14 of the season, have you taken some time to evaluate your schedule, routine, coaches, and players. Are you okay?

Have you taken some time to put God into the daily rhythm of the season?
Where is He with regards to the weekly routine as it involves practice planning and game planning?

Reminders:

How are you in these areas this week? Please take some time to journal on your reminders this week.

1) Power of Words. How were you this week with yours?

____

____

____

2) The Old Iso Play…Who's leading? Man, who's running the show this week? Where are you with that?

____

____

____

3) Don't Worry About Vulnerability. Did you give somebody a portion of you this week? Where are you with that?

____

____

____

Remember:

1) Day 1, pray before the staff game planning meeting. Remove yourself and fill God in.

2) Day 2, pray before the scouting report meeting with the team. See Reminders!

3) Day 3, pray before meeting with position group. See Reminders!

4) Day 4-5, pray with position group for the remainder of the week to help you and the guys remain grounded. If it's about Him, make it about Him in all areas. Not just sometimes. This is a great way to start practice.

Season Week 15
Mystique and folktales never won anything!

In the 60s, you had the Green Bay Packers, in the 70s, the Pittsburgh Steelers, in the 80s, the San Francisco 49ers, and in the 90s, you had the Dallas Cowboys. They were all tough, nasty in the trenches, and found ways to win. When you saw their colors, those helmets and those men coming out of the locker room, you associated all of that with success! Much like the early days of Mike Tyson's professional boxing career when he'd stand in his corner sweating in the pre-fight announcements with his black trunks, no socks, and black shoes on, you were typically beaten before the fight began. Championships have never been won off the backs of reputation, mystique, or talk. Effort, hustle, persistent passion and grind hoist trophies and wear rings! So how did these men gain so much success, consistently, beyond effort, hustle and passion? They gained it through salt! Salt? Yes, I said it, salt.

In Matthew 5:13-16, Jesus spoke about us being salt and light. He spoke about man being salt and not losing flavor. He spoke about how our light should be placed on a stand to give light to everyone. He finally said that our good deeds should shine for all to see so it can praise our Heavenly Father! These men undoubtedly were salt and light for each other in the locker room, in the coach's office and in the community. There was single mindedness throughout the program, the franchise and the team. When programs, traditions and teams begin to fade, look for the salt or the lack of it. Was the flavor lost over time?

Successful programs and franchises are built through re-teaching the importance of developing men with flavor, or shall I say, SALT! There has to be something about you that makes you endure through the whistle and through the fourth quarter. The logo on the helmet, the long line of titles from the previous years, the reputation, are all a benefit from work but more importantly the salt of the man in the uniform. As you prepare your team for the biggest challenge that the end of the season brings in your playoff, bowl game and title run, don't look across the sideline getting engulfed in what you see. Their mystique and folklore won't beat you. They still have to play to earn it like you do. Focus on the salt that's inside the men on your sideline. Look at the worth and value and pull out the flavor from each of your men!

Scripture

Matthew 5:13-16

13 You are the salt of the earth. But what good is salt if it has lost its flavor? Can you make it salty again? It will be thrown out and trampled underfoot as worthless.

14 You are the light of the world – like a city on a hilltop that cannot be hidden.

15 No one lights a lamp and then puts it under a basket. Instead, a lamp is placed on a stand, where it gives light to everyone in the house.

16 In the same way, let your good deeds shine out for all to see, so that everyone will praise your heavenly Father.

Prayer

Father God, help me to not focus on anything I see or the history composed of the men across from me. Help me to focus on the value You created in our men. Help us to develop from the salt You put in us. Thank You for giving us flavor; let us go out and give our very best for You. In Jesus Name. Amen.

Thought process for the week:

As you head into Week 15 of the season, have you taken some time to evaluate your schedule, routine, coaches, and players. Are you okay?

Have you taken some time to put God into the daily rhythm of the season?

Where is He with regards to the weekly routine as it involves practice planning and game planning?

Reminders:

How are you in these areas this week? Please take some time to journal on your reminders this week.

1) Power of Words. How were you this week with yours?

____

____

____

2) The Old Iso Play…Who's leading? Man, who's running the show this week? Where are you with that?

____

____

____

3) Don't Worry About Vulnerability. Did you give somebody a portion of you this week? Where are you with that?

____

____

____

Remember:

1) Day 1, pray before the staff game planning meeting. Remove yourself and fill God in.

2) Day 2, pray before the scouting report meeting with the team. See Reminders!

3) Day 3, pray before meeting with position group. See Reminders!

4) Day 4-5, pray with position group for the remainder of the week to help you and the guys remain grounded. If it's about Him, make it about Him in all areas. Not just sometimes. This is a great way to start practice.

Season Week 16

Dead Silence

Have you ever been in a quiet locker room? Not a sound can be heard except for the music from the band in the stadium or from the stadium PA system that you can still hear through all the cinder block. You can faintly hear sniffles and crying while spat is being torn off and thrown to the floor. It's over and it's practically dead silent in the room. You don't know what happened because it all happened so fast. There's a finality to the moment. The season is over and all that remains is dead silence. Before that quiet moment, you were given inspiration in another quiet moment. It could've been days, weeks, and months before the game. Let me explain!

There was a man in the Bible, named Gideon, who probably had a "dead silence" moment when God instructed him into battle with the Midianites who were more than 130,000 strong fighting men! Gideon had 32,000 fighting soldiers, but God knew there were some men that weren't willing to fight. They were timid, weak minded and didn't possess a "Championship Mindset." Can you imagine the quiet in the room when God instructed Gideon that after 22,000 scared men abandoned the scene, the 10,000 that remained to fight was still too much? Gideon was in his preseason at that moment. The game – the battle – hadn't even taken place yet, but God was qualifying Gideon for a championship run by getting his roster ready. Gideon had to be in full obedience mode at this moment or a loss was bound to take place. Please read chapters 7 and 8 in the book of Judges for the details of how this battle played out.

Believe it or not, before you ever experienced the "dead silence" of a devastated and defeated locker room, you were met with some decisions. God gave you some instructions. You were given the ingredients for success and much like Gideon, you were confronted with a decision to be faithful to His instructions or to say, "that's too much," "it's crazy," or "I can't do that." I've had some restful nights interrupted by God's inspiration at 3 a.m., writing down detailed instructions on a coaching method or a God-inspired thought for the team. I was confronted with a choice of going back to bed in hopes that I'd remember it in the morning or I'd get up at that very moment He inspired me to write down that thought. I've experienced both over the years; times when I listened and times

when I didn't follow through.

Before we can ever taste a "championship," we must first get the recipe for success during our time with God in dead silence. To get all that you've asked God for, please remember the following in your "dead silence" moment with God:

- Listen to God
- Write down inspired thoughts
- Do not over think inspiration, but act on it
- Losses aren't in your DNA; they're building blocks
- Going to battle with appointed men, not old friends

Your greatest inspiration occurs long before chaos. God is birthing you with His master plan of preparation. It's up to us to seek Him and ask for a fine-tuned ear ready to follow instructions. You ask your players to do the exact same thing, so why not you? As you enter your championship game, bowl game, or the last games of your NFL season, remember to get all of God's instructions. Seek quietness for clarity so His plan will be implemented in how you prepare the men He's made you responsible for.

Scripture

Judges 7:3-8

3 therefore, tell the people, 'Whoever is timid or afraid may leave this mountain and go home.'" So 22,000 of them went home, leaving only 10,000 who were willing to fight.
4 But the Lord told Gideon, "There are still too many! Bring them down to the spring, and I will test them to determine who will go with you and who will not."
5 So Gideon took the men down to the water. There the Lord told him, "Separate those who lap the water with their tongues as a dog laps from those who kneel down to drink."
6 Three hundred of them drank from cupped hands, lapping like dogs. All the rest got down on their knees to drink.
7 The Lord said to Gideon, "With the three hundred men that lapped I will save you and give the Midianites into your hands. Let all the others go home."
8 So Gideon sent the rest of the Israelites home but kept the three hundred, who took over the provisions and trumpets of the others."

Prayer

Dear God, thank You for Your inspiration. Forgive me for the times I didn't write down or follow through on Your master plan for this coaching career You've blessed me with. Light a flame in me to be alert even in the darkest of night and quietest morning hours. Help me to write it down, implement it, and exercise all the inspiration you've asked me to carry out for these men. Teach me how to win first with being obedient to You regardless of the circumstances. In Jesus Name. Amen.

Thought process for the week:

As you head into Week 16 of the season, have you taken some time to evaluate your schedule, routine, coaches, and players. Are you okay?

Have you taken some time to put God into the daily rhythm of the season?

Where is He with regards to the weekly routine as it involves practice planning and game planning?

Reminders:

How are you in these areas this week? Please take some time to journal on your reminders this week.

1) Power of Words. How were you this week with yours?

____

____

____

2) The Old Iso Play…Who's leading? Man, who's running the show this week? Where are you with that?

____

____

____

3) Don't Worry About Vulnerability. Did you give somebody a portion of you this week? Where are you with that?

____

____

____

Remember:

1) Day 1, pray before the staff game planning meeting. Remove yourself and fill God in.

2) Day 2, pray before the scouting report meeting with the team. See Reminders!

3) Day 3, pray before meeting with position group. See Reminders!

4) Day 4-5, pray with position group for the remainder of the week to help you and the guys remain grounded. If it's about Him, make it about Him in all areas. Not just sometimes. This is a great way to start practice.

Season Week 17
Alignment & Assignment

After the Christmas holidays, if you are still playing for a prize in this particular season, you are in rare company. You're either an NFL team with destiny on your mind, trying to stay healthy and seeking a rhythm headed into the playoffs; or you're at a university blessed with the opportunity to play for a National Championship or looking to finish the season on a high note with a bowl win to help bolster your recruitment in January for your potential National Championship run.

Whatever category you're in, you indeed stand in rare company this time of year. It's a blessing after 18 weeks to still be standing. The greatest skills a player must have after 18 weeks is trust and his ability to listen. The body has been through the rigors of a long season and both muscle memory and focus tend to fade for some that have been in trench wars all season.

In 2003, the famous Atlanta rapper and entrepreneur, Ludacris, wrote a song called, "Stand Up." The hook in the song was simply, "When I move you move... just like that." As a coach, I'd like to think I understand the importance of alignment and assignment even this late in the season. The hook from Ludacris' song is so much the same thing God requires of you no matter our aches, pains or circumstances in life. He's got the game plan and He needs you to be in the best position to receive the reward for listening and being focused. Yeah, you're tired; yeah, you're sore; but you're almost at the end and the end is what you've been playing for all season long, so don't slow down now!

In 1st Chronicles 11:10-25, the author talks about King David's "Thirty Mighty Men." In verse 11 of 1st Chronicles, chapter 11, Jashobeam used his spear to kill 300 enemy warriors and Abishai. In verse 20, he did the same thing by using his spear to slay 300 enemy warriors. In verse 23, Benaiah wrestled away a spear from a 7 ½ foot tall Egyptian warrior and killed him with it. This group, the "Thirty Mighty Men," truly understood their assignments on the team as well as where they needed to be aligned in battle! The fact that some of these men fought warriors who were 7 ½ feet tall and fought back the enemy, even when outnumbered, showed their commitment to their Godly alignment and assignment.

As you lock it down for this stretch run to determine your place in history, remember your alignment and your assignment. Be what God has called you to be by being the warrior He chose you to be. Many don't make it into this territory this late in the year. Wake up! Be refreshed, there's more to do. Don't take the moment for granted. Go be God's Warrior. You can rest when the season is over!

Scripture

1 Chronicles 11:20-25

20 Abishai, the brother of Joab, was the leader of the Thirty. He once used his spear to kill 300 enemy
warriors in a single battle. It was by such feats that he became as famous as the Three.
21 Abishai was the most famous of the Thirty and was their commander, though he was not one of the
Three.
22 There was also Benaiah son of Jehoiada, a valiant warrior from Kabzeel. He did many heroic deeds,
which included killing two champions of Moab. Another time, on a snowy day, he chased a lion down into
a pit and killed it.
23 Once, armed only with a club, he killed an Egyptian warrior who was 7 1/2 feet tall and who was
armed with a spear as thick as a weaver's beam. Benaiah wrenched the spear from the Egyptian's hand
and killed him with it.
24 Deeds like these made Benaiah as famous as the three mightiest warriors.
25 He was more honored than the other members of the Thirty, though he was not one of the Three. And
David made him captain of his bodyguard."

Prayer

Heavenly Father, thank You for the privilege to still be coaching this late in the year. It's an honor and I'm grateful for it. Teach me to coach, encourage, and set the example of one of your elite Fighting Men. No matter the circumstance, help me to lift your warriors up that surround me. Strengthen me to maintain a laser focus to finish strong. In Jesus Name. Amen.

Thought process for the week:

As you head into Week 17 of the season, have you taken some time to evaluate your schedule, routine, coaches, and players. Are you okay?

Have you taken some time to put God into the daily rhythm of the season?
Where is He with regards to the weekly routine as it involves practice planning and game planning?

Reminders:

How are you in these areas this week? Please take some time to journal on your reminders this week.

1) Power of Words. How were you this week with yours?

---

2) The Old Iso Play…Who's leading? Man, who's running the show this week? Where are you with that?

---

3) Don't Worry About Vulnerability. Did you give somebody a portion of you this week? Where are you with that?

Remember:

1) Day 1, pray before the staff game planning meeting. Remove yourself and fill God in.

2) Day 2, pray before the scouting report meeting with the team. See Reminders!

3) Day 3, pray before meeting with position group. See Reminders!

4) Day 4-5, pray with position group for the remainder of the week to help you and the guys remain grounded. If it's about Him, make it about Him in all areas. Not just sometimes. This is a great way to start practice.

Post Season Self-Assessment
"Identifying the Mike"

Proverbs 4:25

Look straight ahead, and fix your eyes on what lies before you.

While most teams have cleaned out their lockers and headed home for the off-season, you are still here. Next up? Is probably your mantra.

Take this time to identify the "Mike LBer." Just like a quarterback must identify Mike for the sake of knowing the "tells" of the coverage, blitz and core behavior of the defense; you have to remain steadfast this time of year. Identify what is at the heart of your being and use that to drive your position group from this week onto the next.

Football is not a complex game. It is a simple game if taught in a manner that helps a player understand his role. At the end of the day, what you hope for is that the core fundamentals of your player is strong enough to rely on when the game is on the line.

In the scripture, Proverbs 4:25, to start this Post Season Self-Assessment, the author of Proverbs, Solomon, didn't say to focus on everything around you, behind you, above you, in the stands, or in the press box. Proverbs 4:25 says to fix your eyes on the things in front of you. Fix your focus right now! Stick with the routine core fundamentals that brought you this far. Simply put, ID the Mike.

In 2010, I spent a month with the Indianapolis Colts as a Quarterback Coach Intern. This was my first stint in the NFL and I spent my days listening and observing Peyton Manning. He went through his pre-snap process by first identifying the Mike linebacker. He didn't ID the DB or the DT, he identified the Mike. Upon identifying the Mike, the riddle of the defense was solved.

As you've worked your way through this devotional and have read through the weekly workbook, you should've noticed that the journaling doesn't change. It's the core of the devotional, it's the aspect of you spiritually identifying the Mike. Your words and your weekly process is your fundamental routine with God. Continue that this week. Let's go!

Post Season Week 18
Regimented Routine...not Superstition

Your day has arrived, the game is upon you. Routine, routine, routine; not superstition, horoscopes, or magic! Forget the same glass you've been drinking out of in the morning that you haven't washed out since your last major victory, or the same shirt you've worn from 13 years ago that is stretched with a few holes under both armpits from the championship team you played on, or the routine you go through the night before eating the same foods, watching the same shows while going to bed at the exact same time. (These are a few pre-game superstitions I've heard of before game day.)

The Merriam's Dictionary definition of the words superstition, regimented and routine are as follows:
- Superstition: a belief or way of behaving that is based on fear of the unknown and faith in magic or luck
- Regimented: to organize rigidly especially for the sake of regulation or control
- Routine: a regular way of doing things in a particular order

I've been fortunate to have worked for some great men who understood a regimented routine. Instead of worrying about their individual actions before game day or how "stepping on a sidewalk crack would break your momma's back" would affect the outcome of the game, they created an environment where they rigidly organized a particular order for doing things to gain entry to success on the field and off.

In everything we practiced, it was to prepare, direct, and instruct our players to be in the best mental and physical position on the field. Our players were required to run everywhere on the practice field not because it was a cool thing to do but it prepared them to play fast and relentless. Our players were required to arrive early in the mornings on playoff days and eat as a team not because the kids loved chicken, but because it kept the team together and orderly prior to heading on the road. It allowed us to create an environment of single-mindedness before the game. Our players were asked to be involved in winter workouts to test their mental and physical fortitude, not because it brought luck, but because it brought success to the program.

In everything you do, please know that a regimented routine prepares players for battle and directs them towards success. Superstition is for magicians; routine and regiment is God's intentional qualification steps for success. Don't spend another minute doing crazy things with your rabbit's foot. In all you do, do it because God promised you success by you simply following Him.

Scripture

1 Timothy 4:7

Have nothing to do with irreverent, silly myths. Rather train yourself for godliness;

Prayer:

Dear Lord, I have been blessed to be in such a great profession! Teach me Lord to not disrespect You by following myths or superstitions. Strengthen me daily to follow the plan for success that Your Holy Spirit has put on my heart a long time ago, late at night and early in the morning when You were laying out the plan for my success for these men. Strengthen me to recollect all the building blocks You set in place long ago for me as the games become more significant down the stretch. In Jesus Name. Amen.

Thought process for the week:

As you head into Week 18 of the season, have you taken some time to evaluate your schedule, routine, coaches, and players. Are you okay?

Have you taken some time to put God into the daily rhythm of the season?

Where is He with regards to the weekly routine as it involves practice planning and game planning?

Reminders:

How are you in these areas this week? Please take some time to journal on your reminders this week.

1) Power of Words. How were you this week with yours?

____

____

____

2) The Old Iso Play…Who's leading? Man, who's running the show this week? Where are you with that?

____

____

____

3) Don't Worry About Vulnerability. Did you give somebody a portion of you this week? Where are you with that?

____

____

____

Remember:

1) Day 1, pray before the staff game planning meeting. Remove yourself and fill God in.

2) Day 2, pray before the scouting report meeting with the team. See Reminders!

3) Day 3, pray before meeting with position group. See Reminders!

4) Day 4-5, pray with position group for the remainder of the week to help you and the guys remain grounded. If it's about Him, make it about Him in all areas. Not just sometimes. This is a great way to start practice.

Post Season Week 19
Toughness

The definition of toughness, in the Merriam-Webster's Dictionary, is being able to withstand great strain without tearing or breaking; strong and resilient. The material science definition states that it's the ability of a material to absorb energy and plastically deform without fracturing.

In the book of Daniel, Chapter 6, Daniel was another tough man who endured jealousy to the point of being thrown into a lion's den as a death sentence. Daniel never flinched in fear or wavered in his faith. He understood the value God saw in Him and He knew God had better plans despite being put in a man-made death trap. Much like the material science definition of toughness, Daniel didn't fracture as he absorbed the negative energy from his enemy. The Bible says, he didn't have one scratch from being thrown into a den of ferocious hungry lions. That's toughness!

True toughness in life starts when you see yourself the way God sees you; tough and built exactly as an image of Him. You weren't created with wimp tendencies; those were picked up somewhere and are a byproduct of fear. If you somehow mistakenly picked it up, you can get rid of it. That is not an authentic, God-designed trait. If you have children, you can better understand the mindset of what God sees in you. Whether you're a father of boys or girls, you always view them as winners because you helped create them to win in life. From the time they were born, you refused to see them as nothing short of tough because you shaped them to be that way.

That's exactly God's parenting plan for you. He didn't raise you to be anything less than that. Be what God's called you to be by being the tough man He chose you to be. Don't take the moment for granted, be refreshed; there's more to do. Nothing else – I mean nothing else – matters but the moment you're in because it is this moment's purpose that qualifies you for the next one. Tough men understand this principle and never look up for a moment of self-glorification.

There's work to be done and more bricks to be laid. Toughness is more than muscle

flexing, it's a mindset God shaped. It's sustaining, maintaining, absorbing and being unshakable, unbreakable and resilient. Let Him shape you today by sustaining regardless the situation and trusting in a tough God for your next chapter!

Scripture

Daniel 6:19-23

19 Very early the next morning, the king got up and hurried out to the lions' den.
20 When he got there, he called out in anguish, "Daniel, servant of the living God! Was your God, whom you serve so faithfully, able to rescue you from the lions?"
21 Daniel answered, "Long live the king!
22 My God sent his angel to shut the lions' mouths so that they would not hurt me, for I have been found innocent in his sight. And I have not wronged you, Your Majesty."
23 The king was overjoyed and ordered that Daniel be lifted from the den. Not a scratch was found on him, for he had trusted in his God."

Prayer

Father God, thank You for making me tough even when I may fall short of being that way in my mind. Help me to not only live as a tough-minded man, but Lord help me to encourage others around me to be tough in all they do because this is how you shaped our lives to be. Help me to see myself the way you see me. In Jesus Name. Amen.

Thought process for the week:

As you head into Week 19 of the season, have you taken some time to evaluate your schedule, routine, coaches, and players. Are you okay?

Have you taken some time to put God into the daily rhythm of the season?

Where is He with regards to the weekly routine as it involves practice planning and game planning?

Reminders:

How are you in these areas this week? Please take some time to journal on your reminders this week.

1) Power of Words. How were you this week with yours?

____

____

____

2) The Old Iso Play…Who's leading? Man, who's running the show this week? Where are you with that?

____

____

____

3) Don't Worry About Vulnerability. Did you give somebody a portion of you this week? Where are you with that?

____

____

____

Remember:

1) Day 1, pray before the staff game planning meeting. Remove yourself and fill God in.

2) Day 2, pray before the scouting report meeting with the team. See Reminders!

3) Day 3, pray before meeting with position group. See Reminders!

4) Day 4-5, pray with position group for the remainder of the week to help you and the guys remain grounded. If it's about Him, make it about Him in all areas. Not just sometimes. This is a great way to start practice.

The Pause Before the Championship Weeks: Championing a Vision

With every bridge that I've crossed on my journey in this coaching profession, I remember pivotal people along the way. As I learned a few years ago from Nick Savage, a very good friend and mentor, "In this profession, considering your growth already and where you want to go, you're gonna need someone that's going to be your champion. This is strictly a relationship business and someone is going to have to champion your growth. You're not going to get there based on your knowledge and expertise alone."

In 2007, I was invited to the NFL Players Association (NFLPA) Office for lunch by an old friend and the wheels were set in motion for a vision that God had been carving out for me for quite some time. Up to that time, I wrestled with opportunities to do more as a coach. When my daughters were two and three years old, I passed on an opportunity to be a graduate assistant for Coach Mack Brown at the University of North Carolina. The late, great J.D. Hall was a mentor of mine at North Carolina Central University and he forwarded my name to a top assistant at North Carolina. Not understanding the magnitude of the opportunity, I passed on it because I had to continue in my IT career to provide for my family. Fifteen years later, there in that NFLPA Office, someone else besides my wife, saw my capabilities and challenged me to do more.

On this rainy Thursday afternoon in late November, I met Scottie Graham. Scottie looked across his desk and said, "Coach, I watched one of your games in Loudoun at Briar Woods and listening to you now talk about your approach to teaching QBs let's me know, you're not a high school coach. You talk like a college and NFL coach and remind me of some of my old coaches at Ohio State." Scottie was a RB at Ohio State in the early 90s and played in the NFL as well, most notably for the Minnesota Vikings. His statement was resounding for me and set me on a path.

I followed the script he recommended in writing coaches I respected in the NFL. Two of those letters drew a response within a month of me sending them. One from the Pittsburgh Steelers and the other from the Indianapolis Colts. Years before I spent time with Coach Kirby Wilson at the Cleveland Browns, he was a top assistant with the Pittsburgh

Steelers and the other from the Indianapolis Colts. Years before I spent time with Coach Kirby Wilson at the Cleveland Browns, he was a top assistant with the Pittsburgh Steelers. He was kind enough to respond to my letter to Coach Mike Tomlin, encouraging me to reapply for the internship the following year. He conveyed that he was impressed with my information and my desire to grow in the NFL. His words of encouragement to reapply was all I needed to continue this push towards more.

Jim Caldwell, the Indianapolis Colts OC and QBs Coach in 2008, called me upon receiving my letter and remembered me from my first meeting with him at Hampton University one year earlier at a football clinic. I'll never forget his words when he called me, "What is it that I can do to help you in your career path?" As I sat in my office, I actually looked out the window to see if it was a prank. I didn't lose track of the moment. I told him where I wanted to go and what I wanted to do with my career. His willingness to call me and respond to my letter turned into him offering me an internship two years later.

While Scottie Graham was a champion in helping me set the course and Jim Caldwell provided the actual opportunity, there were a few people that helped while I was in the rigors of it all during my year with the Cleveland Browns.

John Wooten, legendary Cleveland Browns player and founder of the Fritz Pollard Alliance, was a champion for my cause in furthering my NFL coaching aspirations. He knew I was coming from the bottom up. He conveyed to me that there aren't many coaches (unless they played in the NFL) that ascend from the high school ranks but he wanted to help. Since 2011, he's mentioned me to a variety of NFL teams. His effort has always been appreciated and in 2017, his reference to the Cleveland Browns, didn't fall on deaf ears. He championed me and helped me get in the door with the Browns. It was up to me to make the most of the opportunity.

I knew it was God's will for me to be in Cleveland by the people he placed in my path while serving the organization. At the time, Coach David Lee was the Quarterbacks Coach and while he was a veteran Quarterback Coach he wasn't fond of the technology tools some coaches used to make the job easier. Coach Lee saw my ability to use the tools

that helped speed up and make our work more efficient. While I served Coach Lee with all of his Quality Control needs, he provided me an education with how to identify NFL defenses, specifically coverages. Coach Lee didn't need me for his Quarterback teaching, but spending time with him daily allowed me to see how he approached his job while learning more definitively the NFL game, as well as the complexities of NFL defenses and how Quarterbacks can survive with all of the details they have to have on a daily basis. God enabled Coach Lee to be a champion for me by recommending to the head coach that I stay and continue to serve in my capacity as a Quarterback Assistant.

While I spent time in Cleveland, unlike my time in Baltimore at Morgan State where I had affordable housing near the campus, I had to pay my way in Cleveland and I had no transportation. I lived in Towneplace Suites, which was an extended stay and used Uber every day to travel to the facility. I didn't want to draw attention while I was on this leg of my journey, so I tried not to ask for anything because I considered it a privilege to have this opportunity to work in the NFL. Each morning started with an Uber ride into the practice facility at 5:15 a.m. I used the Uber every day for almost five months until a great legend in the game found out.

On a cold November morning, Coach Al Saunders greeted me when I walked into the facility from my Uber drop-off. I didn't want to lie to him when he asked me about my mode of transportation, so I told him. I told him I wanted to come and do my job without asking for anything because I knew my purpose in being with the team. He told me that he'd pick me up from that point on because it was on his way. My last two months with the team were awesome for many reasons because Coach Saunders championed my journey and, in addition to practicing this level of kindness, he gave me wisdom on his coaching philosophy and his journey in the profession.

Coach Saunders started his career in 1970, the year I was born. It was humbling everyday to listen to him. I listened and took in all that he offered. I don't think he ever realized how much I valued those rides and sharing that time with him. He provided input in the offensive meetings and made some of my work easier. He was indeed a champion while I was on this part of my journey and it was easy to listen to him because he reminded me of my late father with his wit and daily question to me, "Hey John, you still like football?" I think he'd ask that question every day just to see if I was still hanging on. As simple as

the question was, it was always thought provoking and I'd convey to him a resounding yes, no matter how difficult the day may have been.

No matter where you are in your coaching career, it's important to understand that at some point, you're going to be challenged with the opportunity to champion someone. If you truly believe that God has blessed you to be in this profession, understand that your gift comes with a great deal of responsibility in paying it forward. It was never intended for us to sit on our blessings. It's never about us, but rather about God being served in what we do best.

In Matthew 25:14-30, Matthew talks about "The Parable of Talents." After you review this book of Matthew, you'll understand how important it is to not sit on your talents or under utilize them. We are to give of ourselves and when God presents us the opportunity to "champion" someone else in this profession, it is our responsibility – our mandate – to do so. This is how coaches grow and it's also how our talents increase, as it talks about in Matthew 25. We not only help someone else, but we grow and become better for it.

Post Season Week 20
The Quality of Starting: "Go build the boat!"

Coaches, "Go build the boat!" It's the beginning of the off-season for football programs all across the country. Only a handful of teams remain in competition for the ultimate prize, the Super Bowl. For the rest of us, at every level the vision has been given. The plan is in place and if you're truly listening, the course is being plotted out daily. Whether it's the weight room, plyometrics, speed work, character & mental development '101', or simply goal setting by way of discussion and planning, it's all being formulated now with an end goal in mind. The end goal is designed by the vision and the vision is given by God. If you're truly listening, you're on a course much like Noah was in the Bible.

In Genesis 6:19-22, Noah was not only a great listener but he followed the specific details in God's instructions for what was coming. In Genesis 7:4-5, the Bible speaks of what was coming for the earth. After Noah heard it, he did everything that was commanded of him.

As you "go build the boat!," here are some steps to remember:

- There's a process before the execution. Your moment to, "Go build the boat" is right now. This is the season of preparation.

- Listen for God's direction and wisdom. Noah did exactly what God asked of him even when it was frowned upon, criticized or ridiculed. God will reward your obedience so remain steady, not shaky.

- Be specific and trim the fat now. God called Noah to bring pairs, male and female, on the arc he was building to ensure that life would survive on the earth once it was restored after the flood. God was specific with His order. As a coach, you can take it a step further and trim the fat now. Everyone can't go on this journey through the end of this year. You need those committed to the plan in place to remain and those who are who are not, to stay behind.

As we discussed how vital it is to endure, it's just as important to have the obedience that Noah had and follow the plan God has laid out for the team He's positioned you to oversee. As you head into an off-season of transition, remember to "go build the boat" for the great journey in late July. Take nothing for granted, listen for instruction, execute the instruction, be specific in carrying it out, and trim the fat now.

Scripture

Genesis 6:19-22

19 Bring a pair of every kind of animal – a male and a female – into the boat with you to keep them alive during the flood.
20 Pairs of every kind of bird, and every kind of animal, and every kind of small animal that scurries along the ground, will come to you to be kept alive.
21 And be sure to take on board enough food for your family and for all the animals."
22 So Noah did everything exactly as God had commanded him.

Genesis 7:4-5

4 Seven days from now I will make the rains pour down on the earth. And it will rain for forty days and forty nights, until I have wiped from the earth all the living things I have created."
5 So Noah did everything as the LORD commanded him.

Prayer

Dear God, thank You for the responsibility You've given me to build men. Strengthen me to have a lion's heart and to follow the script You've convinced me to follow. Teach me to remember each day that there's "man's way" and there's "the way." Build me daily Lord to follow "the way," which is the one You've set up for my success. In Jesus Name. Amen.

Thought process for the week:

As you head into Week 20 of the season, have you taken some time to evaluate your schedule, routine, coaches, and players. Are you okay?

Have you taken some time to put God into the daily rhythm of the season?
Where is He with regards to the weekly routine as it involves practice planning and game planning?

Reminders:

How are you in these areas this week? Please take some time to journal on your reminders this week.

1) Power of Words. How were you this week with yours?

____

____

____

2) The Old Iso Play…Who's leading? Man, who's running the show this week? Where are you with that?

____

____

____

3) Don't Worry About Vulnerability. Did you give somebody a portion of you this week? Where are you with that?

____

____

____

Remember:

1) Day 1, pray before the staff game planning meeting. Remove yourself and fill God in.

2) Day 2, pray before the scouting report meeting with the team. See Reminders!

3) Day 3, pray before meeting with position group. See Reminders!

4) Day 4-5, pray with position group for the remainder of the week to help you and the guys remain grounded. If it's about Him, make it about Him in all areas. Not just sometimes. This is a great way to start practice.

Post Season Week 21
Championship Mindset

Imagine it's the last official game of the season, the Championship! You've qualified to get here, but getting here isn't the end goal. Only one will be remembered. On this particular night, your offense has been in a phone booth for almost the entire game. During the regular season your offense averaged 41.4 points a game and on this night, it hit a snag. The defense you're facing has been pressuring you all night long. The defensive line either seems too quick or too strong and for the last 58 minutes they got a little more "dog nasty" in them than your guys! Your starting left tackle was hurt in the first half and is playing with a separated shoulder BUT he's still fighting. Making matters worse is that he's playing against the league's best defensive end. While getting constant pressure on your quarterback, the defense you're facing has played a ton of man-free disguising blitzes along the way while keeping the safety seven yards from the box to stop your running back who is the best in the league. He's fought for every one of his 74 yards on 31 carries. Your quarterback wants to take advantage of the eight man box, but it seems nearly impossible as you face the league's best defense. BUT you've got one more chance. With a minute and 34 seconds left, you still have a chance as you are only down 17-13 on the plus 47 yard line. Your BUT has kept you in the game. What's next? How is this going to play out?

In the book of Luke, there were a group of men who stood tall for a fellow man's circumstance. This group of men in Luke 5:18-20, were carrying a paralyzed man on a mat to Jesus for healing. Things didn't look encouraging upon arriving to the home where Jesus was doing his work. It was crowded to the point where the men couldn't get to Him but that didn't stop them. They worked their way to the roof of the home where Jesus was and removed tiles from a section of the roof. They lowered the man down on the mat down through the hole they created just to get to Jesus. Wow, unbelievable! No, believable! These men refused to be denied. Truly these men had to have been teammates, friends, or brothers of some type, right? There was a connection and a commitment to win!

Quality men are injected with a championship mindset and adversity is the fuel that feeds them. Denial means only delay for them, not finality! They possess the championship

They possess the championship mindset. But what is the championship mindset?

- It's Believing when there's no evidence to believe... It's Faith!
- It's Visualizing what a successful finish looks like because they envisioned it long before the game.
- It's Finishing no matter how bad you're hurting. You keep going and you do it like it's the last time you'll ever do it!
- It's the BUT when all looks bleak, lost, and troublesome. BUT because of Jesus, you know it's never over!

We need to be soaked, bathed, and lathered in the championship mindset. We need to take on the urgent mindset of these men who stood tall for their brother in Luke 5:18-20.

Finish your final drive with the Championship Mindset! It's now 23 seconds left in the game, you've marched from the plus 47 yard line all the way down to the 8! You've converted three third downs along the way and are knocking on the door. You're in scoring position. Believe in what God has promised you. Believe, visualize, finish, and know that God's BUT let's you know it's not over.

Scripture

Luke 5:18-20

18 Some men came carrying a paralyzed man on a mat and tried to take him into the house to lay him before Jesus.
19 When they could not find a way to do this because of the crowd, they went up on the roof and lowered him on his mat through the tiles into the middle of the crowd, right in front of Jesus.
20 When Jesus saw their faith, he said, "Friend, your sins are forgiven.

Prayer

Dear Lord, thank You for the faith to finish! I pray for a Championship Mindset in supporting every man you've put alongside me to support. Strengthen me to always be willing to carry my brother on to victory no matter the odds before us. In Jesus Name. Amen.

Thought process for the week:

As you head into this last game, the championship game, you've earned the right to be in this exclusive club. Are you ready? Have you kept the "main thing, the main thing"? If you have, you've already accounted for your coaches, players, and staff. Remember to take that time with God during this last week of the season. Check to make sure you've taken some time to evaluate your schedule, routine, coaches, and players. Keep the main thing the main thing. The game should be a byproduct of God's blessings. Make sure you are focused on Him. Are you okay?

Have you taken some time to put God into the daily rhythm of the season?

Where is He with regards to the weekly routine as it involves practice planning and game planning?

Reminders:

How are you in these areas this week? Please take some time to journal on your reminders this week.

1) Power of Words. How were you this week with yours?

____

____

____

2) The Old Iso Play…Who's leading? Man, who's running the show this week? Where are you with that?

____

____

____

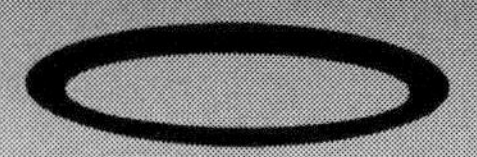

3) Don't Worry About Vulnerability. Did you give somebody a portion of you this week? Where are you with that?

____

____

____

Remember:

1) Day 1, pray before the staff game-planning meeting. Remove yourself and fill God in.

2) Day 2, pray before the scouting report meeting with the team. See Reminders!

3) Day 3, pray before meeting with position group. See Reminders!

4) Day 4-5, pray with position group for the remainder of the week to help you and the guys remain grounded. If it's about Him make it about Him in all areas. Not just sometimes. This is a great way to start practice.

Postseason Self-Assessment "Finishing"

Romans 8:28

And we know that God causes everything to work together for the good of those who love God and are called according to his purpose for them.

God gave your season a purpose. You made it! Now that you are at the end of this season, a list of things confront you. Whether you're thinking about preparation for next season with the team or leaving the team for another opportunity – no matter the scope of the reflection point you're on right now – do it with decency. God created a place for you, so don't let your character slip. Whether you're leaving or returning for another opportunity to improve the team, write down and identify where you first can improve. As God said in Habakkuk, write down the vision! It's imperative to put on paper the plan going forward and to use it as a point of reference.

Habakkuk 2:2-3

2 Then the LORD said to me, "Write my answer plainly on tablets, so that a runner can carry the correct message to others.
3 This vision is for a future time. It describes the end, and it will be fulfilled. If it seems slow in coming, wait patiently, for it will surely take place. It will not be delayed.

Things to remember:

1. What did you do to bring harmony?

2. What can you do to improve yourself holistically and as a coach? Simply put, scout yourself.

3. Consult with a mentor to provide feedback on areas where you can improve. Remember, a mentor will be someone who will call you on the carpet.

4. If you're not returning, leave with dignity and honor as God's man. Don't leave cutting

the ropes to the bridge behind you. If necessary and possible, mend relationships before walking away.

5. Leave the names out of it. Don't damage your character by speaking poorly of another coach or player. If it's not positive, eat it. It's not worth it and that can play negatively on your future destination

6. Eat it, refer to #5. Check the ego in the coat closet and leave it there.

7. Thank God for the opportunity to be an impact on others. Now plan for the new season and the move forward. Start by creating a theme scripture and memory verse for the new season for you and your position group. It's time to reload!

Coach as if God is in the stands!

About John Tomlinson

John Tomlinson was born on November 25, 1970 in Baltimore, MD to Irene Nora Schulz and John Tomlinson Sr. John was raised by his father John Sr. from the tender age of 2 years old and didn't see his mother again until he was 18 years old.

John was raised in Prince Georges County Maryland and graduated from Frederick Douglass High School in Upper Marlboro, MD in 1989. He then went to Winston-Salem State University on an academic scholarship and graduated in 1993 with a B.S. in Computer Science and a minor in Math. He began an Information Technology career in Research Triangle Park, NC before moving to Virginia.

John started his coaching career in 1994 at Cardinal Gibbons High School in Raleigh, NC. He later traveled down the highway to Hillside High School in Durham, NC where he was the OC and QB coach in his last year before returning to the Washington D.C. area and working as a QB Coach and OC at various schools.

Most notably, Coach Tomlinson assisted in turning around the program at Falls Church High School in 2000 and 2001. He then helped start a new program at Briar Woods High School from 2005 to 2008, transitioning them from a JV program to being ranked 7th in the state of Virginia before accepting a new challenge in 2009 and moving to Texas.

Upon arriving in Texas, Coach Tomlinson worked at Southwestern Assemblies of God University in 2009 as a RB Coach. In 2010, he left Texas and took an internship as a QB Asst with the Indianapolis Colts. This served as a life changing moment as he was mentored daily by Head Coach Jim Caldwell, Coach Frank Reich, Coach Gene Huey and Coach Tom Moore. It set a direction for how he coaches QBs.

In 2012, Coach Tomlinson was the QB Coach and Quality Control Coach at Morgan State University in Baltimore, MD. He helped build a top-five recruiting class in the FCS that year and improved a stable of young QBs. In 2013, Coach Tomlinson took a coaching position with the Cedar Hill High School football program in Cedar Hills, Texas. He was an Assistant QB Coach, having shared in the success of two state championships in 2013 and 2014. In addition, he was the QB Coach and Co-Passing Game Coordinator in 2015 and 2016. In 2017, he began an internship with the Cleveland Browns, which provided the opportunity for him stay on staff as an Assistant QB Coach and Quality Control Coach.

Coach Tomlinson is married to Kathy Tomlinson and has four children: Kenny, Amesha, Imani, and Kirsten.

Made in the USA
Lexington, KY
01 August 2019